Finding Confidence in Times of Trial

Finding Confidence in Times of Trial

Letters of St. John of Avila

Translated and Selected from the Spanish
by the Benedictines of Stanbrook Abbey

Preface by the
R.R. Abbot Gasquet, O.S.B.

SOPHIA INSTITUTE PRESS
Manchester, New Hampshire

Finding Confidence in Times of Trial: Letters of St. John of Avila was originally published under the title *Letters of St. John of Avila* in 1904 by Burns and Oates, Ltd., London. This 2012 edition by Sophia Institute Press includes minor revisions.

Copyright © 2012 Sophia Institute Press

Printed in the United States of America

All rights reserved

Cover design by Carolyn McKinney

On the cover: *Juan de Avila,* c. 1746 (oil on canvas),
by Pierre Subleyras. © Birmingham Museums and
Art Gallery / The Bridgeman Art Library.

Sophia Institute Press
Box 5284, Manchester, NH 03108
1-800-888-9344
www.SophiaInstitute.com
Sophia Institute Press® is a registered trademark of Sophia Institute.

Library of Congress Cataloging-in-Publication Data
John, of Avila, Saint, 1499?-1569.
    [Correspondence. English. Selections]
    Finding confidence in times of trial : letters of St. John of Avila /
       translated and selected from the Spanish by the Benedictines of
       Stanbrook ; with preface by the R. R. Abbot Gasquet.
       p. cm.
    Originally published: London : Burns and Oates, 1904. With minor
       revisions.
    ISBN 978-1-933184-83-8 (pbk. : alk. paper) 1. John, of Avila, Saint,
       1499?-1569.--Correspondence. I. Stanbrook Abbey. II. Title. III. Title:
       Letters of Saint John of Avila.
    BX4700.A78A25 2012
    282.092 — dc23

                                   2012010912

Contents

Preface

This little volume contains the translation from the Spanish of a few spiritual letters of St. John of Avila. The author is probably not much known to English readers; certainly he is not as well known as he deserves to be both for his own merits as a writer and because in his own time, the sixteenth century, and even beyond the limits of his own country, Spain, he was a man of great renown. He was recognized everywhere as a special servant of God, and as a true director of all souls desiring to walk the higher paths of perfection, or of those who needed help and encouragement to serve God in the humbler walks of life.

He was also a preacher of exceptional power. St. Francis of Sales[1] in his *Practice of the Love of God* speaks of him as "the learned and saintly preacher of Andalusia," St. Francis Borgia[2] as "the Great Master," and he was popularly known as the "Apostle of Andalusia" from the wonderful change his preaching wrought in that district of Spain. His discourses were likened to "fishermen's nets gathering in fishes of all sorts" whenever and wheresoever he cast them, so plentiful was the harvest of souls that followed his expositions of the Christian teaching.

---

[1] St. Francis de Sales (1567-1622), Bishop of Geneva.
[2] St. Francis Borgia (1510-1572), Duke of Gandia who became a Jesuit, established the Jesuit order throughout western Europe, and sent missionaries to America.

Finding Confidence in Times of Trial

It may perhaps seem somewhat strange that one endowed by God with such personal holiness and who had been called to guide the souls of St. John of God, St. Francis Borgia, St. Peter of Alcantara, and St. Teresa[3] should have had to wait so long a time before being raised to the ranks of the formally beatified servants of God. It is fortunately not in any way necessary for us to explain such apparent neglect; but it was only on the twelfth of November 1893, some three centuries and a half after his death, that Pope Leo XIII, of happy memory, decreed his Beatification, and the faithful were invited to invoke his protection and aid under the title of Bl. John of Avila.[4] The writings of the great servant of God have hitherto been little known, at least in England, and it is with the confident expectation that those who will read the letters here printed will find in them spiritual comfort and solid Christian teaching, that they have been translated from the Spanish.

For the sake of those into whose hands this little volume may fall, who are unacquainted with the life of St. John of Avila, it may be useful to give a brief outline of his career. Letters and other writings of anyone wholly unknown to us do not as a rule interest us as much as when we have at least a general knowledge of their author and of the circumstances under which they were written. From a contemporary historian we learn that our author was born on January 6, 1500, at Almodovar del Campo, a town in the diocese of Toledo and in the kingdom of New Castile. Spain was then under the rule of Ferdinand and Isabella, and the Church was governed by Pope Alexander VI.

---

[3] St. John of God (1495-1550), founder of the order of the Brothers Hospitallers; St. Peter of Alcantara (1499-1562), mystic and founder of a reformed order of Franciscans known as the Alcantarines; St. Teresa of Avila (1515-1582), Spanish Carmelite nun and mystic who reformed the Carmelite order.

[4] John of Avila was canonized on May 31, 1970 by Pope Paul VI. — ED.

The parents of St. John of Avila were people in a good social position and able to give him an excellent education, but more important than this, they were both truly and solidly pious. In fact, their son was given to them in their old age when they had ceased to hope for children, as the direct result of prayer during a pilgrimage made in honor of St. Bridget.

From his early boyhood, St. John of Avila manifested signs of extraordinary piety, and it required little discernment to see that God had destined him for some special service in the Church. At the age of fourteen he had finished his literary studies and as, in the opinion of his masters, he gave promises of a distinguished career, his father sent him to the University of Salamanca to study law. After a twelvemonth spent in the legal schools, however, he manifested such a distaste for secular studies that his father allowed him to return home. The next three years were spent almost entirely in the seclusion he made for himself, with the consent of his parents, in his father's house, and in which he devoted himself to the practice of penance and to the study of the science of the saints with our Lord and His Blessed Mother as his chief teachers.

At the end of this period of retirement, by the advice of a friend, he determined to prepare for the priesthood. With this intention he went to Alcala to commence his philosophy and theology, which he was fortunate enough to be able to study under the celebrated Dominican professor de Soto, who formed the highest opinion both of his abilities and of his exemplary piety. While here, he formed a lasting friendship with Don Pedro Gerrero, who afterward became Archbishop of Granada and to whom several of his letters are addressed.

Before he had finished his philosophical course, both his parents died. He remained on at the university until his studies were sufficiently advanced for him to receive the sacred Order of Priesthood, when he returned home to say his first Mass in the church wherein his two parents were buried. After this, he disposed of his family property and gave the proceeds to the poor. The desire of his heart inclined him to the missions in Mexico and, having no family ties and having dispossessed himself of all his belongings, he seemed to see in his circumstances an indication of the divine will in his regard. He consequently made all preliminary arrangements and repaired in 1527 to Seville to await an opportunity of setting out for the scene of his mission. Meantime his days and nights were spent in prayer and penance and in filling his mind with that heavenly learning which only constant communing with God Himself can impart.

The design formed by St. John of Avila of leaving Spain to work in the Mexican missions was not, however, destined to be carried out. At the beginning of 1528, he was induced by ecclesiastical authority to renounce the idea in order to assist in evangelizing the province of Andalusia.

His first sermon was preached on July 22, 1529. He had looked forward with dread to the ordeal of facing an audience and speaking to them of the high mysteries of God and of their duties as Christians. As he mounted the pulpit, his nervousness for a few moments deprived him of the power of speech, until he remembered that it was God's work, undertaken only for His sake, and raising his mind and soul to heaven he said: "My God, if it be Thy will that I should preach, remove from me this great confusion I am feeling. Do this, I beg Thee, by the memory of Thy bitter Passion, for Thou knowest whether I seek aught else but Thy glory and the salvation of souls." At once his nervous distress passed away, and he became one of the most eloquent and successful preachers that Spain has ever seen.

Whenever it was known that he was to preach, the church was thronged by crowds anxious to hear him, and great harvests of souls were gathered wheresoever he sowed the seed of the word of God. Fr. Luis of Granada, who wrote his life likened him to an arquebuse[5] loaded to the very muzzle, which made great havoc at every discharge.

Many instances are given in his life of the effect of St. John of Avila's sermons. The two most celebrated examples were undoubtedly the conversions of St. John of God and of St. Francis Borgia, which were wrought by the power of his preaching. The former, a Portuguese traveling merchant, came by accident in 1537 to a place where the holy servant of God was preaching and by the effect of his burning words was changed from a worldling with no higher thoughts than those of his business into a man given to heroic and lifelong penance.

The change wrought in St. Francis Borgia was equally astonishing. In 1539, Queen Isabella died at Toledo after a few days' illness. Francis Borgia, Marquis of Lombay, who had been a member of the royal household, was chosen to escort the body to Granada for burial. On the arrival of the body, the coffin had to be opened in the presence of Borgia, for the formalities of identification, when the terrible change that had been wrought by the hand of death in the features of the once beautiful queen was seen by Borgia and made a great impression upon him. St. John of Avila was appointed to preach the funeral oration and, as if inspired to enforce the lesson already taught the courtier by the sight of the corrupted body of his former mistress, he spoke in forcible terms of the transitory character of worldly honor and position, and of the corruption that overtook all mankind alike and from which neither king nor prince could escape. His words wrought the instant conversion of St. Francis Borgia and by St. John of Avila's advice, he joined the Society of Jesus as one of the first disciples of St. Ignatius.[6] For this great saint and for his new Society, which was founded at this time, our venerable servant of God always entertained the warmest affection and admiration.

[5] An early firearm.
[6] St. Ignatius of Loyola (1491-1556), founder of the Jesuit Order.

He sent many of his disciples to the Jesuits and encouraged them in the many difficulties and troubles experienced by them in their first beginnings in Spain. One of the letters printed in this little volume is addressed to Dr. Loarte and to another person, on their becoming Jesuits; another is a letter of consolation to a dying son of St. Ignatius, and a third, to friends undergoing persecution, is also perhaps sent to encourage some members of the Society in their troubles. In the then need for Christian education and religious instruction in Spain, St. John of Avila regarded the foundation of the Society of Jesus as a marked instance of God's providence in providing for the wants of the Church. His opinion was communicated to St. Ignatius and was a source of great satisfaction and consolation to him. Moreover St. John of Avila gave so many practical proofs of his desire to assist the Society in its early days that he was accounted its best friend in Spain and for all the foundations made by the Institute in Andalusia it was directly indebted to his influence.

For some years before his death, St. John of Avila suffered from constant sickness, which, however, he did not allow to interfere with his working for souls. He bore his maladies in the spirit of gratitude to God, who allowed him to suffer something for his love—the spirit he so earnestly exhorted others to cultivate, as in the two excellent letters addressed to people who are ill, which are printed in this volume. After sixteen years of suffering St. John of Avila died on May 10, 1569.

Some of the works of this venerable servant of God have never been published, such as his "Treatise on Clerical Life" and his "Remarks upon the Council of Trent." Of his published writings his "Spiritual Letters," and his tract "*Audi Filia*" are the best known. Both were translated into English in the seventeenth century: the "*Audi Filia*" in 1620 by L.T., and the "Letters" in 1631, but these editions, especially the English translation of the letters, have long been very scarce books. Even had they been easily obtainable, their antiquated diction and the involved nature of the translation would make them antiquarian curiosities rather than books practically useful for spiritual help at the present time.

The letters with which we are immediately concerned are very numerous. In the French translation of Robert Arnaud d'Andilli, they are divided into four sections or books; the first contains letters (twenty-two in number) addressed to prelates and other religious superiors; the second (thirty-one in number), those written to nuns and superiors of convents; the third (sixty-three in number), letters to women of quality in the world; and the fourth (thirty-three in number), those to laymen of all kinds.

The present selection of twenty-five letters has been made from the entire number and affords examples taken from all four divisions. Although only a small number, they will be sufficient to give the reader some knowledge of the power and charm of St. John of Avila's epistolary style. Moreover they set forth, better than any life can, the personality of this great servant of God. The letters of all great and good men are a precious inheritance to those who come after them, and they afford information about their inner souls and an insight into the working of their minds, which can be obtained in no other way. The Benedictine editor of the letters of St. Augustine[7] explains exactly wherein consists the special value of the documents he was engaged upon. "As the eyes are to the other bodily senses," he writes, "so are the letters of illustrious men in numberless ways more wonderful than all their other works ... Just as no one can better show himself to the life than in his letters, so nowhere can he be better known than in them ..." Any careful reader may, in such letters, look into the soul of the writer as if he were close at hand.

Luis de Munoz, who is the author of one of the Spanish lives of St. John of Avila, devotes a considerable space to the letters

---

[7] St. Augustine (354-430), Bishop of Hippo.

written by this servant of God and to the spirit which dictated them. From early youth, this servant of God, he says, set St. Paul before him as a model and became the living image of the great Doctor of the Gentiles, imitating him in his actions, preaching, and virtues, and indeed fulfilling the apostle's command: "Be ye imitators of me as I am of Christ."[8] Munoz then goes on to point out how this imitation of St. Paul was manifested in the letters written by St. John of Avila. Just as the apostle, whose burning zeal was not quenched with preaching to those who could hear his voice, endeavored in his epistles to draw all the world to Christ, so St. John of Avila, his disciple and humble imitator, wrote an immense number of letters to all sorts and conditions of people. He had no idea of composing a volume of letters, nor could he have dreamed that what he penned would ever have been published, but providentially at least some of them were preserved so that later generations might enjoy his earnest exhortations and profit by the spiritual food intended originally for the person or persons to whom the letters were actually addressed.

It is impossible not to admire the style and vigor of the letters here printed. The doctrine taught in them is solid and fruitful, and their persuasive quality speaks for itself. The words, says Munoz, have such power and force that they fire the most frozen and the hardest of hearts, and nobody can read them without wishing and resolving to change his life for the better. Many learned and pious theologians have looked upon these letters of St. John of Avila as among the most precious of the many writings of God's saints and have declared that for them alone, in their opinion, he would deserve to be called a Doctor of the Church. And indeed St. John of Avila's whole manner of writing is that of some early Father of the Church whose aim was to secure, not the good of his own individual soul, but that of the whole Body. His versatility

---

[8] 1 Cor. 11:1.

is extraordinary and he seems to enter fully into the difficulties that are proposed to him, although the subjects upon which he is asked to write are as numerous, and as different, as were the needs of the people who applied to him for advice.

Fr. Luis Munoz writes:

> With what convincing and powerful reasons does he not console the sad, encourage the weak, rouse the tepid, strengthen the timid, help the tempted, weep with the fallen and humble the presumptuous? How admirable is his unmasking of the arts and tricks of the enemy! What wise counsels he gives for defending ourselves against him! What clear indications and signs he sets forth by which a man may know whether he is advancing or falling back in his service of God! How he shows the weakness of the strength of nature and the power of grace! How clearly he exposes the vanity of the world, the malice of sin, and the ever-present dangers of this life! With what eloquence and insistence does he not exhort us to put all our trust in the fatherly care of God and in the merits of the Precious Blood of Christ! How efficaciously he urges upon us the virtue of patience in trials, cheers us in sorrow, and encourages us in afflictions and troubles! There is no state of life in the Church of which he does not make known the special duties and the means by which they may be fulfilled. He tells great lords how to govern their vassals and manage their estates: he instructs priests how worthily to offer the Holy Sacrifice, and preachers how to preach with fruit, and he shows virgins espoused to Christ how to guard zealously their purity.

If such is the character of these spiritual letters, we need not wonder at being told that St. John of Avila never wrote to anyone without producing a wonderful effect in the soul of the recipient, leading to a permanent change and improvement of life. Fr. Munoz tells us that St. John of Avila wrote his letters with extraordinary ease and rapidity. As a rule, he wrote down just what occurred to him without any previous thought or study. Generally the letter was sent just as it was first written off, without obliterating or correcting anything, and those who knew him ascribed the facility with which he set forth his arguments, gave his advice, and enforced them by the words of Holy Scripture and of the Saints, to the prayer to which he gave himself each morning.

Sometimes, however, he would not reply to a communication at once. On such occasions, he would say : "Let us recommend the matter to our Lord and say Mass about it." Days might pass without a reply being sent, and if he were pressed to send an answer he would say, "Our Lord has not yet told me what to say to you." Then, after a time, he would write with as great a certainty and clearness as if he had heard the answer from our Lord Himself.

We are told in the life of this holy servant of God that the Society of Jesus always particularly esteemed and appreciated his works, and in some Jesuit houses in Spain, they were read in the refectory during a considerable portion of the year. In Lent, the "*Audi Filia*" was chosen, because it treated so sublimely of the Passion of Christ. During the Octaves of Pentecost and Corpus Christi, St. John of Avila's sermons on the Holy Spirit and Corpus Christi were read, and during a good part of the rest of the year, his *Letters*, "so full of spiritual prudence."

Sufficient and more than sufficient has been said about the *Letters* of our holy author, for after all, they will speak their own praise best. One word, however, may be permitted about the translation itself. Those who are responsible for it have, in my opinion rightly, endeavored to reproduce in English the force and charm of the original thought, without necessarily copying the words exactly or translating the Spanish idioms and phrases in too servile a manner. Their aim has been to give to English readers the idea of the author rather than the actual words in which, according to the genius of his own beautiful Spanish tongue, he was constrained to express it. The following passage from Cardinal Newman exactly states the principles that have guided the translators in their work:

As to the translations, he [Newman] is very sensible what constant and unflagging attention is requisite in all translation to catch the sense of the original, and what discrimination in the choice of English to do justice to it; and what certainty there is of shortcomings, after all. And further, over and above actual faults, variety of tastes and fluctuation of moods among readers, make it impossible so to translate as to please everyone; and if a translator be conscious to himself, as he may well be, of viewing either his original or his version differently, according to the season or the feeling in which he takes it up, and finds that he never shall have done with correcting and altering except by an act of self-control, the more easy will it be for him to resign himself to such differences of judgment about his work as he experiences in others.

It should be considered, too, that translation in itself is, after all, but a problem; how two languages being given, the nearest approximation may be made in the second to the expression of ideas already conveyed through the medium of the first. The problem almost starts with the assumption that something must be sacrificed; and the chief question is, what is the least sacrifice? In a balance of difficulties, one translator will aim at being critically correct, and he will become obscure, cumbrous and foreign; another will aim at being English and will appear deficient in scholarship. While grammatical particles are followed out, the spirit evaporates; and, while an easy flow of language is secured, new ideas are intruded or the point of the original is lost, or the drift of the context impaired. Under these circumstances, perhaps, it is fair to lay down that while every care must be taken against the introduction of new, or the omission of existing, ideas, in translating the original text, yet, in a book intended for general reading, faithfulness may be considered simply to consist in expressing in English the *sense* of the original; the actual words of the latter being viewed mainly as *directions into* its sense, and scholarship being necessary in order to gain the full insight into that sense which they afford; and next: that where something must be sacrificed, precision or intelligibility, it is better in a popular work to be understood by those who are not critics than to be applauded by those who are.[9]

F. Aidan Gasquet
Stanbrook Abbey
Feast of the Invention of the Holy Cross
May 3, 1904

---

[9] "Advertisement" to *Historical Sketches*. vol. 2.

Finding Confidence in Times of Trial

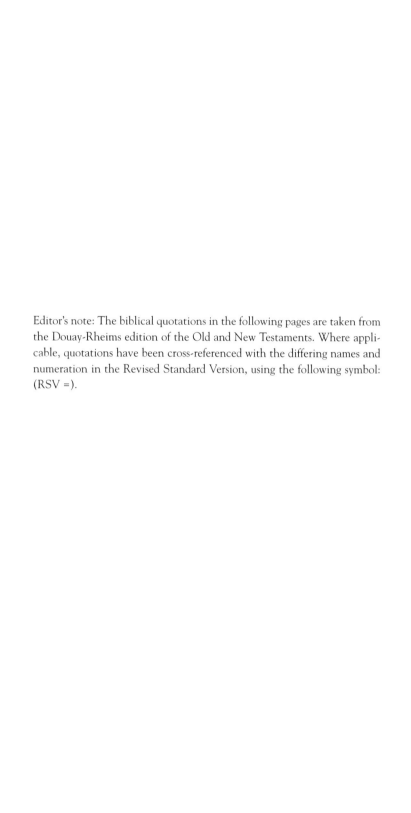

Editor's note: The biblical quotations in the following pages are taken from the Douay-Rheims edition of the Old and New Testaments. Where applicable, quotations have been cross-referenced with the differing names and numeration in the Revised Standard Version, using the following symbol: (RSV =).

To St. Teresa of Avila

On True and False Visions

St. Teresa was led by God along such extraordinary paths and granted so many sublime and miraculous favors as to cause the saint herself, as well as many other people, to fear that she was deluded by the devil. She consulted several theologians who were unable to agree on the subject, and the Inquisitor Soto de Salazar advised her to write a clear account of her spiritual life and prayer and submit it to the judgment of St. John of Avila, "who" he said, had "so much experience and authority that, if he approves of your book, your mind may be set at rest forever." This narration of the saint constitutes the well-known Life of St. Teresa, Written by Herself, *which is considered by the Church a standard treatise on mystical theology. The following favorable reply from St. John of Avila, made probably about 1563,[10] brought her great comfort, as she tells us in her letters. On hearing of his death, St. Teresa wept, saying, "The Church has lost one of her chief pillars, and many souls are deprived of a guide and support, of whom I am one."*

May the grace and peace of Jesus Christ our Lord be ever with you. I consented to read your book, which was sent me, not so much

[10] A mistake has been made in the date prefixed to this letter. The Madrid edition of Fuente, published in 1881, gives it as September 12, 1568, which is probably correct.

because I considered myself competent to judge of such matters, as because I thought that, by the grace of God, its teaching might benefit me. Although I have had no leisure to study it as thoroughly as it deserves, yet, thanks be to God, it has given me great consolation, and it will be my own fault if it does not profit my soul. On my own account, it might suffice to say no more about it, yet I think the gravity of the subject and the respect due to the person who sent it require me to express my opinion of it, at least in general terms.

It is not a book proper for everyone to read—the language requires to be corrected in some places and to be made clearer in others. There are things in it which, although useful to you in your own spiritual life, would not do for everyone to practice, for God guides some souls along extraordinary paths that are not intended for others. I have noted most of these passages and will arrange them for you as soon as possible, and send them to you without fail. If you knew the infirm state of my health, and how I am constantly employed in many necessary duties, you would, I am sure, be more inclined to pity me than to accuse me of neglect.

On the whole, your teaching on prayer is correct, and you may safely trust to it and practice it; the raptures, too, afford proof of being genuine. What you say about God's teaching the soul without the use of the imagination—that is, by interior or exterior communications—is safe, and I can find no fault with it. St. Augustine treats this subject well. Such communications, both interior and exterior, have misled many in our times; the exterior ones specially are less safe; for though there is little difficulty in knowing that they are not from ourselves, it is not so easy to decide whether they proceed from a good or from an evil spirit. There are many rules for discovering when they come from God; one is that they should come to us in times of need; or be a great help to the soul, such as strengthening it in times of temptation or doubt; or warning it of the approach of danger. For if even a man who is good never speaks without purpose, how much less would God do so. Considering that the communications mentioned in your book are conformable to the Holy Scriptures and the teaching of the Church, I judge that, if not all, at least the greater part of them come from God. Visions, whether imaginary or corporeal, are the most deceptive: they are never to be desired, and, should they come uninvited, they should, as far as possible, be resisted. Unless, however, it is certain that they proceed from an evil spirit, this should not be done by making signs of contempt. I was pained and shocked to hear of its having been done in your case. We should beg of God not to allow us to walk by sight, but to defer the revelation of Himself and His saints until we reach Heaven, and we should ask Him to guide us while on earth along the common path by which He leads His faithful friends.

We must also take other suitable means for shunning these visions. If, nevertheless, they continue to come to us and are profitable to the soul, not inciting her to vanity, but increasing her humility; if, moreover, these communications be conformable to the teaching of the Church, and if they last a considerable time and infuse a spiritual joy into the soul that can be better felt than described, I do not think that it is necessary any longer to try to avoid them. No one, however, should be his own guide in these cases, but should communicate them at once to some enlightened counselor. This is the universal rule to be followed on all such occasions, and we may trust that God will not suffer anyone to be deceived who wishes to be safe and has the humility to acknowledge his incompetence to judge in such matters for himself.

It is not right, however, to cause alarm, and at once condemn these favors because the soul to whom they are vouchsafed is not perfect, for, as I have often witnessed, God withdraws people from harmful pleasures, and even from grievous sins, by sending them His sweet consolations. Who shall place limits to God's mercies? As these graces, moreover, are not bestowed on anyone on account of his own merits or strength but, on the contrary, are often given to souls because of their weakness, they neither necessarily increase sanctity, nor are always granted to the greatest saints. It is unreasonable for anyone to disbelieve these matters because of their sublime nature, or since it appears incredible that a Majesty so exalted should abase Himself to hold such loving intercourse with His creatures. It is written that "God is love"[11]—and if He is love, He must needs be infinite love and *infinite* goodness, and it is no wonder that such love and goodness should at times bestow on certain souls an affection that confounds those who do not understand it. Although many know this by faith, yet, unless they have experienced it themselves, they cannot understand the affectionate, and more than affectionate, way in which God elects to treat some of His creatures. Those who themselves are far from having received favors of this kind cannot believe God would deal with others in so different a manner. Yet it would be only reasonable to think that such love, a love that fills us with wonder, must come from God, who is marvelous in all His works, but still more marvelous in His mercies. But what should really be a proof of the truth of these favors (provided other circumstances confirm the evidence) is taken by some people as a pretext to deny their reality.

From your book it is clear that you have resisted in these matters even more firmly than necessary. These graces have evidently benefited you, especially by showing you your misery and faults and helping you to correct them. They have continued for a long time and always profited your soul, moving you to love God and despise yourself and to do penance. I am therefore more inclined to think these favors beneficial than to condemn them, if you are cautious, and do not blindly trust to them, especially those of an unaccustomed kind, or those that urge you to perform any action doubtfully good. In cases such as this, you must suspend

[11] 1 John 4:16.

your belief in them and at once seek counsel. I warn you that, although these graces should be sent by God, the devil might mingle falsehood with them; therefore always be on your guard. Even though it be certain that the favors come from God, do not let your mind dwell on them with complacency, for holiness does not consist in such things, but in a humble love of God and our neighbor. Fear all ways other than this, and practice humility, the virtues, and the love of our Lord.

Do not worship any of these visions, but only our Lord Jesus Christ, either in heaven, or in the Blessed Sacrament. If one of the blessed should appear to you, raise your heart to that saint in Heaven and not to what you see before you: let the image lead your thoughts to the reality. The things of which you treat in your book happen to many souls in these times, and there is no doubt that they proceed from God, whose arm is not shortened so that He cannot do now what He did in past ages: He chooses the weaker vessels the better to manifest His glory.

Continue in this path then, but be watchful against robbers and pray for guidance. Thank God for having given you a love for Him, a knowledge of yourself, and an attraction for penance and for the cross. Do not concern yourself much about the other matters, although you should not despise them, for many show signs of coming from God, and the rest can do you no harm if you ask direction about them. I cannot believe that I have written this by my own power, for I have none, but it is the result of your prayers. I beg you for the love of Jesus Christ our Savior, to pray for me to Him: He knows that I need it urgently, and I feel sure that is enough to make you grant my request. I must beg you now to let me conclude, as I am obliged to write another letter.

May Jesus be glorified by all and in all!

Your servant for Christ's sake,

Juan de Avila

2

To Don Diego de Gusman and Dr. Loarte on Becoming Jesuits

Rules for Living a Holy Life

Fr. Diego de Gusman and Dr. Loarte were amongst the earliest disciples of St. John of Avila to enter the Society of Jesus.

The former, who may be called his firstborn spiritual child, was son of Count Baylen, but renounced his rank and wealth in early youth to become a priest. He spent fifteen years in preaching with great fruit and was then, in 1552, received into the Society of Jesus by St. Francis Borgia. He continued his former work until called to Rome by St. Ignatius Loyola, who sent him to preach in different parts of Italy. He died in Andalusia with the reputation of a saint.

Dr. Loarte was a famous theologian and assisted Fr. Gusman in his work in Spain, but his great humility made him choose the office of catechizing children and hearing confessions. They were received together into the Society of Jesus and went to Rome at the same time. Dr. Loarte was later made head of the college at Genoa and died in Spain in 1582.

I. Do not select any particular means for promoting your own ends nor fix your affections on any persons, but content yourself with wishing them well and interceding for them to God. Beware of desiring to aid them by any special ways of your own choosing; on the contrary, resist such thoughts as you would a temptation.

II. Do not imagine that you enter the Society to criticize other people, but ever keep in your heart that saying of a holy monk: "I am come to be judged by other men, not to judge them." Be most careful to avoid this danger, especially if you consider yourself wise and enlightened, for it is easy to make mistakes in such matters and even to risk losing divine grace. Believe that God directs those He sets to govern, and that Superiors may have some special motive or intention for their actions of which you know nothing. In short, do not judge other men, and keep clear of all that does not concern you—"What is it to thee? Follow thou me"[12]—otherwise you will live in a state of constant anxiety and trouble.

III. Ground yourself thoroughly in obedience, and consider that God has shown you great mercy in calling you to practice it in this life. Trust that He will make His will known to you through your superiors, having this confidence, not on account of any wisdom they possess, but because He has promised to aid the humble. If you obey implicitly, you will enjoy great peace and make rapid progress in a short time.

IV. Although you are not allowed the liberty you think necessary for you to win souls, but are occupied in duties of a different kind, do not be disquieted on this account. The maintenance and extension of this Order contribute greatly to the salvation of men, which is the object for which it was instituted. Therefore, if you are merely washing dishes, you are helping to convert souls, and you should be perfectly content with such work and should consecrate your life to helping the Society in whatever way you are bidden by those set over you. Do not let your thoughts dwell on any other service, but willingly do whatever is commanded you, not so much for the sake of the merit of the action itself; as

[12] John 21:22.

10

because obedience requires it of you. Consider that Christ has given you a great grace in calling you to be a member of this Society in which He is so fervently served.

V. Be prepared for the cross, and have it ever before your eyes; strive to give no cause for complaint to others, and bear patiently with their faults. Let not differences of character in the various members of the community disturb your mind, for until you have well stood the test of living in the society of your brethren, you must not consider that you have made much spiritual progress. Your principal care should be to live in charity with your brethren, suffering injuries joyfully and willingly; taking example from the meekness of Christ our Lord, let others tread you as the mire beneath their feet. You will meet with so many temptations on this point, that unless you watch vigilantly, you will be certain to fall. Keep your attention fixed on yourself; never argue with or rebuke other people, nor try to rule them, unless the duty is laid upon you: if it is not, let your watchword be: "I am not come to judge but to be judged."

VI. Apply yourself to work at your own progress in the spiritual life with all the diligence proper for accomplishing God's designs. Remember that you have been called to behold the celestial vision of Christ hanging upon the Cross, and that you stand on holy ground; therefore let no immortified affection reign within you. "Be strengthened in Christ and in the power of his might"[13]; deny yourself not only in your senses, but chiefly in your will, and most of all in your understanding, for it is this which saps the foundations of good and is the enemy of peace; this is the presumptuous ring-leader of rebellion and the judge of its superiors; this is the father of divisions and the enemy of obedience, because it is an idol set up in the place of God. Again and again I exhort

[13] Eph. 6:10.

and entreat you, by the mercies of Christ, to humble your understanding and let God reign over it by faith, holding firmly that what your superiors command is our Lord's will. Let this thought and no other be ever your consolation and your refuge in all difficulties, for as long as you hold to it, all will be well with you.

Five grades of humility

The first grade is that, recognizing his own baseness, a man should treat his own will with contempt.

The second is outwardly to show this self-contempt both in dress and manners, and by choosing work of a mean and servile character.

The third is to be patient when despised by others.

The fourth is to rejoice in being despised.

The fifth is to desire with the whole heart to be despised by others.

Twelve other degrees of humility[14]

The first degree is the fear of God.

The second is to deny our own will.

The third is obedience.

The fourth is patience.

The fifth is the confession of sins.

The sixth is contempt of oneself.

The seventh is to prefer others to oneself, esteeming them more highly.

The eighth is to avoid singularity in outward things.

The ninth is to be silent unless spoken to.

The tenth is not to be prompt to laughter.

---

[14] These are a short epitome of the famous twelve degrees of humility, contained in the seventh chapter of the Holy Rule of St. Benedict.

The eleventh is to speak little and with gravity.
The twelfth is to prefer a low estate and occupation.

Ten counsels to lead the soul in the way of salvation

1. At once to reject from your mind not only rash judgments of your neighbor, but the very thought of his faults or sins. Turn your mind toward God and show Him the wounds of your own soul that He may cure them.

2. If you have not the strength to desire sufferings, censures, vexations, or affronts, rudeness and hard work, at least endure them patiently and in silence: do not concern yourself to know from whom they come, but look upon them as sent from the hand of God. Pray to Him for those who are the cause of these trials and beg Him to give you grace to bear them for His love, reflecting that patience in suffering is a sign of salvation.

3. Return thanks to God for all your spiritual graces, natural gifts, and every other good that you possess, attributing nothing to yourself except your sins, faults, and imperfections.

4. When any feeling of jealousy arises in your mind on account of the spiritual, natural, or temporal advantages of your neighbor, lift up your heart to God, begging of Him to increase these gifts in your brethren; rejoice in the well-being of others and be sorry for their shortcomings.

5. Let it be your firm conviction that you should neither desire nor strive for anything but to possess the grace and love of God, to avoid offending Him, and to please Him in all things. Whether death or life, sickness or health, joy or sadness, honor or shame, be your lot—whether you be the

rector or the cook, either here or at the other end of the world—it will matter nothing, except insofar as it brings you nearer to God.

6. Be persuaded of this truth, that as long as you live, you will have to suffer trials, sorrows, temptations, and the cross, for this is the livery of the servants of Jesus Christ our Lord. Bear these patiently, remembering that your sins are many and deserve far greater punishments: "The life of man upon earth is a warfare"; and "He that shall persevere unto the end, he shall be saved."[15]

7. Whenever you give way to any thought, word, or work of pride, such as that you are better, or more useful, or in any way preferable to others, reject it instantly as most abhorrent to God. Confess your sins and faults to Him and beg Him to remedy them: "For God resisteth the proud, but to the humble he giveth grace."[16]

8. When reason tells you that others are guilty of some matter as to which you are innocent, do not excuse yourself, even though you are not blameworthy, but accuse yourself and praise your brother, even if it may bring upon you punishment or reproof or pain. Although upon this occasion you have not deserved it, your past sins have merited this penance; thus, you can never suffer as one wholly innocent, and therefore never exculpate yourself.

9. Frequently during the day, but especially when you make your examination of conscience, remember to render thanks to our Lord Jesus Christ for having redeemed you and made you a friend of God, and for having gained so

[15] Job 7:1; Matt. 10:22.
[16] 1 Pet. 5:5.

many benefits for you by His Passion and sufferings. Bless God for having given Him to you; you should also glorify God for His own perfections.

10. The fruit of Holy Communion and of all other spiritual exercises should be to obtain for us greater strength to serve and love our Lord, to resist temptations, to bear our trials with patience, and not to afford us sweetness or pleasant feelings, which are usually signs of imperfection and may even be sent by the Devil to deceive us. Do not, therefore, strive to gain these sentiments if our Lord does not send them to you, and if He should, beware of presumption by despising your neighbor because he is without them, for, very possibly, he is holier and more dear to God than you are.

Fifteen rules for one who purposes entering the religious state

1. Keep your sins ever before your mind and repent of them daily.

2. Consider yourself most vile and negligent in all things and unworthy of the company or sight of other men, and so, despairing of any good in yourself, trust solely in the mercy of God.

3. Not only must you abstain from judging others, but you must keep your mind solely fixed upon your own faults, so that you may neither perceive nor reflect upon the defects of other people.

4. Neither show nor feel anger toward anyone, nor bear them any ill will or hatred, but keep your heart quiet, peaceful, and humble, and let your demeanor be grave and modest.

5. Show yourself prompt and willing to help others.

6. Use no idle word nor joke, nor speak lightly, unless charity to your brethren demand it.

7. Bear patiently all annoyances, contradictions, abuse, and hard words sent you by God to try you: suffer them cheerfully and even desire them; be resigned and do not let your soul rebel against them.

8. Mortify all desires to know, hear, experience, or possess anything which is unnecessary; let your one earnest effort be to profit your soul.

9. Instantly drive away all thoughts that would lead you from God.

10. Let your only care in this life be to please the Almighty.

11. Do not puzzle over events which happen or wonder why such and such things occur, but take them all thankfully from God's hands, trusting firmly that He watches over you and all men and will never permit anything to happen but for our greater good, however little we may understand it.

12. Be content with the food which is given to the community in general, and do not ask for anything extra as long as you are well. If you cannot eat what is set before you, give thanks for the opportunity of mortifying your appetite.

13. Do not concern yourself about what is no business of yours, particularly in respect to the faults of your brethren or the actions of superiors.

14. Always render obedience, respect, and sincere affection to your superiors; hold them in high esteem, and never

allow anything to be said or done in your presence either against them or other people.

15. Let your soul as well as your body keep solitude; never be idle, and endeavor to despise all earthly things. Diligently observe the rules and constitutions in the proper place, time, and manner, and all other necessary circumstances, for these are the weapons of your warfare, and unless you wish to run the risk of temptation, you must be most strict on this point.

3

To a Beautiful and Popular Woman
Who Chose the Consecrated Life

On the Rewards and Blessings of Holy Virginity

It was the custom in Spain at the time this letter was written, as we often read in St. Teresa's works, for young girls to consecrate themselves to our Lord by a vow of virginity and to live henceforth a life of penance in the world, like the consecrated virgins of the early Church. The letter is probably addressed to Doña Sancha Carillo, a court beauty who, on the eve of a brilliant marriage, made her confession to St. John of Avila and at once decided to renounce the world. She made a vow of chastity and lived a most austere life in a hermitage adjoining her father's house at Quadalcazar. When Andalusia was threatened with famine for want of water, Doña Sancha, at the age of twenty-four, offered herself as a victim to appease Divine Justice so that the country might be spared: God accepted the sacrifice, a time of plenty followed, and the virgin was afflicted with the terrible disease, of which she died on August 13, 1537. It was for Doña Sancha that St. John of Avila wrote his celebrated treatise called "Audi Filia." Her life has been written by Fr. Martin de Roa, S.J.

Devout servant of Jesus Christ,

I cannot find words to express my joy at hearing that you, who might easily have made an advantageous marriage in the world, have resolved to take the King of Heaven for your Spouse. The tidings, although new to me, as I had not been told it, was not altogether unexpected, for I had already secretly chosen you to be consecrated to the Lord, who created you, and I had begged you of Him as a great favor that I might offer you to Him. May His name be forever blessed for granting me far more than I thought of asking. What else was the happiness you felt at having freed yourself from the miseries of this world and at having received the pledge of love from the celestial King, but a sign that your change of plans proceeded, not from your own inconstancy, but from God, who had put the desire into your heart. The happiness came from Him as a testimony and pledge of the many great and pure joys He will give you if you prove faithful to Him. The least of these is incomparably better than husband, children, riches, or anything else this world can give.

Would that you knew by experience how sweet God is to those who forsake created things to gaze on their Creator! How tenderly the Divine Spouse cherishes those who cast away all transitory joys. They are like the chaste turtledoves which refuse all earthly comfort and long only for the love of their Lord in Heaven, and like the dove that returned from her flight from the ark to her master's hand as pure as when she left him, undefiled by having touched any dead body even with her feet. Is anything the world contains of less account than a corpse full of corruption? Why unite ourselves with what will only contaminate us? For the bitterness its joys leave behind is a thousand times greater than any pleasure they give us.

Return heartfelt thanks to Christ for the light to distinguish between the priceless and the worthless, between eternal and temporal things, between God and a mortal man. Be grateful to Him for grace to make the blessed choice and determination to cleave to God and refuse an earthly husband and, for love of a divine union, to reject human wedlock, however advantageous.

Be loyal to Him you choose for your Bridegroom; you will see why He is called the pure Spouse of virgins, and will find all joys in Him. Your union will not resemble earthly marriages, in which a little happiness is succeeded by bitter repentance; not only will it please you at first, but the more you dwell with our Lord, the better you will know Him and the more dearly will you love Him. Christ is not like a man, whose faults we discover on intimacy, as one who appears to be a good husband on the wedding day, but who shortly proves to be one impossible to live with. There is nothing in our Lord to displease us, nor in our Blessed Lady, who is the mother of her Son's brides.

Blessed be the hour in which you took this resolve, and far more blessed the time when your Spouse will visit you with such graces as to make you cry, "O my Lord, how have I deserved to find Thy hidden treasure? A thousand lives would have been too little to give in order to purchase it!" What happy and fortunate espousals! What joy will they not bring both to heaven and earth?

God the Father delights to see souls so love His only-begotten Son as to give up all human affections for Him and renounce not only those pleasures forbidden by His command, but even the lawful tie of marriage. To refuse for Christ's sake what is permissible is a proof of fervent love for Him. The Son is the Bridegroom; He died not only that some might love Him with purity of soul, but that others should consecrate to Him the chastity of their bodies. The Holy Spirit is immaculate and averse to all impurity. When He finds that a soul despises carnal pleasures, He watches over it, fills it with spiritual consolations and never leaves it unsatisfied, since it has refused earthly consolations.

Our Blessed Lady is the Mother of the Spouse, whom she closely resembles, being most loving and benign. She is the Queen of virgins, their protector, and their advocate, and she rejoices to see virginity flourish on earth, for it is the flower she planted there. Nor is the wedding without pages to attend it, for the angels are the servants of the King of Heaven, always ready to do His bidding.

Children, too, which the world so desires, spring from this union; they are born without pain, they give no trouble to educate, nor bring sorrow by turning out badly, or dying young. The children of this marriage are good works, which may well be called the fruit of Christians. What a joy for the soul to conceive the purpose of giving an alms to the poor or of performing some other good works, and to give it birth by practicing it. These children bring both happiness and honor to their mother. She has no need of finding a dowry, for they will bring one rich enough to purchase Heaven for her. They will obtain for her such peace of mind that she will lie down to sleep at night more calm and satisfied than if she were mistress of the earth with all its pleasures.

Now, tell me, what is there in the world, even though worth its weight in gold, that can approach to such gains as these? For one hour of pleasure here, we suffer a hundred hours of pain; and if there exists happiness without alloy, it will not last forever, for either the wife or the husband will die, and so all will end in sorrow. Even if the children do not die first, their mother weeps at parting from them.

Rejoice! then, bride of Christ, for your Spouse is immortal, and at your death, your good works, which are your offspring, will surround you. You will not suffer grief at leaving them, for they will accompany you to God's throne; there they will more than repay all the pain and labor they have cost, and their mother will be welcomed for her children's sake.

Death will not dissolve this marriage, but rather will unite the bride and the Bridegroom closer to one another. Christ will deliver you, for He is the Lord of life and death, and no devil shall dare to touch you, whom God has taken under His protection and honored with the name of Spouse. The angels will come to minister to you and present you to Almighty God; singing praises to Him and calling down benedictions on you, they will say, "Come bride of Christ, and receive the crown He has prepared for thee."

Our Lady, too, will be there, with many other virgins who have gladly trodden the same path on earth. Thus, you will leave this world with your fellow virgins and ascend to the nuptial chamber which our lord has prepared for you, where you will always enjoy riches, plenty, and happiness in the house and in the presence of God. You will be absorbed in incessant contemplation of His infinite beauty; one hour of such joy is a reward greater than could be deserved by all that you have suffered, or that has been, or ever will be, borne by the whole human race. All good things will be yours; you will have reached the end for which you were created and will possess God more fully than can be told or imagined. Your soul will overflow with joy, like one who is in a sea of delights, surrounding him on every side.

Then you will see, praise, enjoy and possess the Lord of all things, and will cry out, "I have Him whom I have loved; I have found Him I sought for. He, for whom I renounced the world has become my wages and my reward, and Him I will praise and love unto endless ages." Amen.

4

To a Priest

*How a Christian Should Prepare for Mass
and Participate in Mass*

*From his childhood, St. John of Avila had a most ardent love for the
Blessed Sacrament of the Altar. He spent two hours every morning
in preparing to say Holy Mass and another hour in thanksgiving; and
sometimes he took two or three hours to celebrate it. His great zeal
for training priests was an outcome of this devotion, and he spared no
effort to inculcate a like affection for this Sacred Mystery on priests
under his direction. During the infirmities of his later years, his greatest relief was to write about the Holy Eucharist, and he has left many
treatises and sermons on this subject.*

Very Reverend Father,

I beseech our Lord that my delay in answering you may be
compensated by the soundness of the doctrine contained in my
letter and by the help it may bring your soul, for your request is
one of serious import and requires a suitable reply.

You wish to know what is the best preparation to make before
offering the most Holy Sacrament of the Body and Blood of our
Lord Jesus Christ, and the most profitable considerations to bear
in mind during the celebration. You ask this because you fear lest,

for want of due dispositions, that which ought to bring great blessings to your soul should injure it instead. Men's bodies, as you know, are of very various temperaments, and there is just as great a dissimilarity in the constitution of their minds, for God bestows very diverse gifts upon different individuals. He does not lead all by the same path; therefore, it is impossible to fix upon any devotion as the most suitable during Mass, but what our Creator and Redeemer puts into the heart and what moves it most to piety is the best.

These things are not matters of faith, and there is no certain rule about them, and if anyone has reason to think that his dispositions and preparation for this Mystery are instigated by God, there is no reason to change from them until our Lord should inspire him so to do. This should be ascertained by laying the matter before some experienced person and following his advice. Some have no special attraction for any one form of devotion at this time, and they, too, ought to consult someone as to their interior dispositions, so as to know whether they should allow themselves to be led by motives of love or fear, of sadness or joy; and how to apply the remedies most suitable to their needs.

From what you have told me about yourself, I consider that you have made progress in virtue, and that it would be best for you to practice yourself in considerations proper to excite in you fervent love and reverence. For this purpose, I know of nothing better than to meditate on the fact that our Lord, with whom we are to treat, is both God and man, and to think over the reasons for which He comes down upon the altar. Surely such a stroke of love[17] should be enough to awaken anyone from the slumber of indifference. Let such a one reflect upon this Mystery and say to

---

[17] At the mere mention of the Blessed Sacrament, St. John would often exclaim, with tears coursing down his cheeks: "O great stroke of love! O great stroke of love!"

himself: "It is God Almighty who will come down upon the altar at the words of Consecration: I shall hold Him in my hands, and converse with Him, and receive Him into my breast."

If only we remember this, and if, by the help of God's Holy Spirit, it penetrates our soul, it will suffice, and more than suffice, to enable us, frail mortals as we are, to perform this sacred duty as we ought.

Who can help being inflamed by love on thinking that he is about to receive the Infinite Goodness within his bosom? Who would not tremble with reverential fear in that Presence, before which the powers of Heaven are awed? Who would not resolve never to offend Him, but to praise and serve Him evermore? Is it possible for anyone not to be confounded and overwhelmed with grief at having sinned against that great Lord whom he bears in his hands? Can the Christian fail to trust such a pledge, or can he want for strength to walk the way of penance through the desert of this world, nourished by such food?

In short, such considerations, by God's help, entirely change and possess the soul, and draw it out of itself—at one time, by feelings of reverence, at another, by love, and yet again, by the strong emotion caused by the realization of Christ's presence. Although these thoughts do not inevitably produce this result, yet unless the heart hardens itself into stone against their influence, they strongly conduce to it.

Let your mind, then, dwell on such reflections; listen to the cry: "Behold, the Bridegroom cometh"[18] — your God cometh! Retire into the secrecy of your own heart, and open it to receive what is wont to come from so powerful a Light. Beseech this same Lord that, as He has deigned to place Himself within your hands, He will give you the further grace to esteem and venerate and love Him as you should. Beg Him fervently not to permit you to be in

---

[18] Matt. 25:6.

the presence of His Majesty but with reverence and fear and love. Endeavor constantly to have a fitting sense of our Lord's presence, even should you contemplate no other part of this Mystery.

Think how men, when they have due respect for the king, stand before him with gravity and reverence, even though they be silent. Better still, picture in your mind how the highest in the court of Heaven behave in the presence of the Infinite Majesty. See how they tremble at the remembrance of their own littleness and burn with the fire of love, so that they appear to be consumed in its furnace. Imagine yourself in the company of these, who are so gloriously adorned, who are so reverent and so fervent in God's service, and being in such society and standing before so great a King, strive to feel as you should at such a time, even though you meditate on no other point. I wish to show you how it is one thing to be able to speak fitly to the king, and another to know how to conduct yourself becomingly in his presence, although you may have simply to stand by in silence.

This is that union with our Lord which should keep you as closely united to Him during Mass as you are in the interior of your heart when alone with Him in your cell, and which will prevent your being distracted by the words you have to pronounce. You must, however, pay fitting attention to the Liturgy, while accustoming yourself at the same time to keep your mind fixed on God's presence. O great God!

What should not be your feelings when you hold in your hands Him who elected our Lady and enriched her with celestial graces to fit her to minister to the God made man! Compare her hands, her arm, her eyes with your own! The very thought should cover you with confusion. What stringent obligations do such benefits lay upon you! What care must you not take to keep yourself wholly for Him who honors you in such a way as to place Himself in your hands, and comes into them when you pronounce the words of Consecration!

These, Reverend Father, are no mere words, nor lifeless thoughts, but they are arrows shot from the strong bow of God Himself, which pierce and wholly transform the heart, so that when Mass is over, the mind ponders on our Lord's words: *"Scitis quid fecerim vobis?* —Know you what I have done to you?"[19] Would that it were possible for a man to understand "what our Lord has done for us" in that hour, and to taste Him with the palate of the soul! Oh, that man had scales that could rightly weigh this benefit! How happy would he be, even in this world! When Mass is over, he would feel a loathing for all creatures; their society would be a torment to him, while his only joy would be to remember "what the Lord had done to him," until he should say Mass again the next day.

If God should ever give you this light, you will realize what shame and sorrow you ought to feel on approaching the altar without it, but he whom it has never illuminated knows not the torture of losing it.

Besides the consideration of *who* it is that comes down upon the altar, you may also meditate on *why* He comes, and you will see a semblance of the love shown in our Lord's Incarnation, Nativity, life, and death, and how these mysteries are renewed in the Holy Sacrifice of the Altar. If you could enter into the very Heart of our Lord, and if He would vouchsafe to show you that the reason for His coming down upon the altar is an impassioned and strong affection, which will brook no separation between the Lover and His beloved, your soul would swoon away before the very sight of such a marvel.

The mind is greatly moved by realizing Christ's presence on the altar, but when it further reflects that He comes to us because His affection for us is like that of the betrothed for his bride, which will not allow him to pass a single day without seeing and

---

[19] John 13:12.

conversing with her, the Christian wishes he had a thousand hearts wherewith to make a fitting return for such love. He longs to cry out with St. Augustine: "*Domine, quid tibi sum, quia jubes me diligere te? Quid tibi sum?* Lord, what am I to You, that You should bid me love You? What am I to You?"

Why do You so fervently desire to see and to embrace me? *You*, who dwell in Heaven in company with those who understand so well how You should be served and loved, come to *me*, who knows only how to offend You or to render You slack service. Can You not, then, O my Lord, be happy without me, that my love should draw You down to me? Oh, blessed may You be, who being what You are, has yet set Your heart upon such a creature as me! Can it be that You, King as You are, come here and place Yourself in my hands, and seem to say: "I died once for your sake, and I come to you now to show you that I do not repent of it, but on the contrary, that, if there were need, I would give my life for you a second time"? Who could remain unmoved by such love? Who could hide himself, O Lord, from Your burning Heart, which warms our own by Its very presence and is like a mighty furnace, throwing out sparks of fire on all around it?

Such a Lord as this, dear Reverend Father, visits us from heaven, and we, wretches as we are, speak with Him and receive Him within our breasts!

Let us now conclude our discourse on this great Mystery, so worthy of being meditated on and understood. Let us beg our Lord that as He has already done us one favor, He will grant us a second, for unless we appreciate His blessings and thank and serve Him for them as He deserves, they will benefit us little. Rather, as St. Bernard[20] says of an ungrateful man: "*Eo ipso pessimus, quo optimus* — The greater his gain ought to be, the greater is his loss."

Let us watch over our conduct during the day, lest Christ

---

[20] St. Bernard of Clairvaux (1090-1153), abbot and Doctor.

punish our faults when we are at the altar. Let us ever bear in mind the thought: "I have received our Lord and sat at His table; tomorrow I shall do the same." By this means, we shall avoid sin and have the courage to do what is right, for our Lord is wont to reward at the altar what is done away from the altar.

To conclude, I would remind you how, when Jesus was the guest of Simon the Pharisee, He complained that His host gave Him no water for His feet, and kissed not His face,[21] to show us that when He enters our house, He would have us wash His feet with tears for our sins and manifest our love as the kiss of peace. May our Lord bestow on you, both for yourself and for your neighbors, this peace, which is born of perfect love, and may you grieve both for your own sins against God and those which other men commit against Him. I pray that you may enjoy this peace one day in Heaven, and also that you may hold God's interests dearer than your own, because of the greater love you bear Him.

I beg of you, for His sake, that if there be aught in this letter which requires amending, you will correct it for me, and thank God for any good it may contain, and I ask you to remember me when you are at His altar.

[21] Luke 7:44-45.

5

To a Widow

On Grief as Spiritual Purification and Renewal

Madam,

I have delayed writing to you, for I thought that my words could do little to mitigate the great sorrow which they tell me you are suffering. It seemed to me that I could help you better by interceding on your behalf with the God of all consolation, than by anything I could say. However, I am strongly urged to send you a letter, and as it is so much desired and our Lord is able to fulfill His purposes even by such means as this, I must not fail to comply with the request. God grant that my words may bring to your heart the comfort I wish it.

It is our Lord's will that you should taste of the sorrows of this vale of tears, and not of the milder but of the most bitter kind. May His name be ever blessed, His judgments adored, and His will fulfilled, for the creature owes its Creator reverence and subjection in all things, be they pleasant or painful. To test our obedience, and to teach us what great things we are bound to do and to suffer for so great a Master, God is wont to deprive us of what is as dear to us as the light of our eyes.

Abraham had a strong affection for his son Isaac, and that was the point on which the Almighty tried him. Job fondly loved his seven sons, and God took them from him in one day. In this manner He treats all those who are dear to Him, that they may testify their love for Him, while He bestows great graces on them by this means.

I know that human nature cannot understand this. It thinks only of the grief and the loss, and cares for nothing else. But if God dwells in us, we must restrain our feelings and make them subservient to reason and to His will. Whatever our suffering may be, we must not let it overwhelm us. Remember our Lord's anguish, which wrung from Him a sweat of blood and made Him cry out: "Father, not my will but thine be done."[22] If we would be known as His disciples, we must say the same, for as His servants on earth, and His companions in Heaven, He will have none but those who take up their cross and follow Him, as sheep do their shepherd, even if the path leads to death.

Tell me, what right have we to complain of our trials, for they enable us to rid ourselves of our sins and make us like to the Son of God? It would be monstrous for slaves to refuse to obey a law their master kept, or for an adopted son to rebel against what the true son bore. Who was ever more beloved by the eternal Father than His only-begotten Son? Yet who was ever afflicted with so many sufferings as He? He was the "Man of sorrows, and acquainted with grief."[23] Count the drops of water in the ocean, and then you may number His afflictions. As the Son of God endured such anguish, being sorrowful even unto death, ought we to pass our lives without tasting one drop of the vinegar and gall with Him? How ashamed should we feel at seeking to share His joys, but leaving Him alone in His agony!

Let none deceive themselves, but let them feel assured that, as the King of Heaven entered His kingdom through tribulations, we must reach it by the same path. There is but one way — "Christ,

[22] Cf. Luke 22:42, 44.
[23] Cf. Isa. 53:3.

and Christ crucified." If we seek a different road, we shall not find it. We should lose ourselves by any other path, and find that, however hard the sufferings of this world may be, those in the next world are far worse.

Oh! blindness of the sons of Adam, who think nothing of the future as long as they can enjoy the present; who care not for what profits them, but only for what pleases them, and subordinate their reason to their passions. They weep when they ought to be glad, and rejoice when they have cause to mourn. Earthly happiness, like smoke, gradually fades away until it is no more seen. The years we pass here are but as a brief dream, from which we awake to find that it has all been an illusion. When sorrow comes to us, however light it may be, we forget our past joys, and the remembrance of them is only grief to us.

If this world is so treacherous a delusion, why not seek the other? Day by day we see our life slipping from us; let us strive for that which will bring us eternal happiness. If, in the past, prosperity has often made us think that we could find happiness here, may our eyes be anointed with the gall of suffering, so as to give us light to see the misery of this world, which is not our own country, but a land of wretched exile. Let us raise our hearts, that our conversation may be in Heaven.[24]

Our Lord has sent you this trial to make you cling closer to Him, since you have less on earth for which to care. Do not fancy that He takes pleasure in your pain, for He is merciful and feels a tender pity for your tears. He has embittered your cup with this drop of wormwood so that, as all human consolation is taken from you, your heart may rest on Him alone. God has deprived you of one happiness only to give you another in its place, as is His wont: He has taken your husband from you, that He Himself may fill his place, for He is called the "Father of the forsaken."

---

[24] Cf. Phil. 3:20.

Finding Confidence in Times of Trial

Your widowhood will bring with it many trials, and you will often miss your husband's care; many of your friends will show you but little kindness or fidelity, and some will even prove ungrateful. When this is so, God wishes you to have recourse to Him and to make Him the confidant of all your trouble. Open your soul to Him as your true Father. If you call on Him with all your heart and trust yourself in His hands, you will find Him a sure refuge in all your difficulties, and a guide on your way. Without knowing how, you will often find that your affairs have succeeded beyond your highest expectations. Experience will show you how true a friend the Almighty is to those in tribulation; how He dwells with them and provides for them. If, sometimes, He does not grant all you desire, it will be to give you something that is better for you; this is how the heavenly Physician treats the sick who go to Him wishing to be cured, rather than to taste pleasant medicines. Do not withdraw yourself from His hands, however painful His remedies may be. Ask Him not to do your will in what He does, but to do His own.

Let your weapons be prayers and tears—not useless tears for what our Lord has taken from you, but life-giving tears, which may gain pardon for your husband's soul and salvation for your own. For what purpose, dear Lady, does the unmeasured grief serve to which they tell me you yield, except to add sin to sorrow? For you know that as we should not indulge in foolish mirth, neither must we indulge in excessive grief; but both in the one and the other we must be obedient to God's holy law.

Why do you complain? Why, I ask, do you complain? Either you are a sinner, and this affliction is to cleanse your soul, or you are righteous, and must be tried, that you may win your crown. Whichever you be, it is right that you should render heartfelt thanks to your Creator, that you should be resolute in loving the end to be gained by your sufferings, nauseous as the medicine may be.

This is what the Holy Scriptures mean when they relate how Esther kissed the top of King Assuerus's rod.[25] Let not the years pass in insatiate sorrow, but lift up your heart to our Lord, and prepare yourself for that passage from life which you have seen others take before. You have already yielded enough to nature; dry your eyes, and spend not the time that was given you to gain eternal life in mourning over death. Remember how our Lord drove from the house those who were mourning the death of a young maiden, saying: "She is not dead, but sleepeth"[26] — in peaceful rest; so does your husband, for he both lived and died a true servant of Christ. Why should you be so grieved because God has taken the man you loved from this unhappy world into the place of salvation?

If it bring you trials, accept them willingly, that your spouse may rest in peace. If his absence afflicts you, take comfort by the thought that you will soon rejoin him, for the days of this life are brief, and it is but of little consequence which of us dies first. It is well to believe that our Lord took him because he was ready for death, and that you have been left here that you may prepare yourself for it. You served God earnestly during your married life; continue to do so now that you live in the state of widowhood; accept its special trials with patience, so that if you gained thirty-fold before, you may now earn sixty-fold. Thus, although your life may not be a very happy one, it will greatly profit your soul, for by it you will purge away your sins, you will imitate Christ on the Cross, and you will hold the certain hope of gaining His eternal kingdom.

To this end, with tears and prayers you must beg our Lord for His grace; you must read books of devotion and receive the Celestial Bread of the most Blessed Sacrament. Raise up your dejected heart and take courage to go on your way; you have a long road to traverse before you can reach Heaven, and you will not arrive

[25] Esther 5:2.
[26] Mark 5:39.

there without suffering more afflictions still. The gem you desire to win is of inestimable value, and no price can be too great to purchase it. God never costs too dear, however much we pay for Him. Rejoice in the hope of possessing Him, for He is one day to be yours. Do not murmur at your troubles, but say: "I look for so great a good to come that I do not feel my present misery." I pray and hope that our Lord Jesus Christ may accomplish all this in your soul.

6

To an Invalid

On the Grace to Be Found in Physical Affliction

Madam,

I have heard of your illness and cannot say I am sorry for it; for if it is caused by excess of penance, it proves that your mortifications have been real, and if our Lord has sent it, it should be welcome as the share He gives you in His Cross. Although, God knows, I am grieved at your pain, on the other hand, I am glad, because it will profit one whose progress I have so much at heart.

I do not desire comfort for my children, but stripes and afflictions; the time for consolation will come hereafter. Ever keep the Cross before your eyes, and unite your heart to Him who placed Himself upon it. Do not be satisfied until suffering becomes sweet to you, for that is the sign of true love. You must not think you are to be pitied; both in Heaven and in this world there are many who have a warm affection for you, and your sufferings come from the loving providence of God.

Let not your faith and love be weakened by your pain and trouble. A large fire is increased, rather than quenched by the wind; so, although a weak love of God is, like a candle, easily extinguished by the first puff of air, true charity gains force and courage by its trials. This is the fire that comes down from Heaven which no water of tribulation can extinguish. Our Lord bids you love Him; this does not allow of self indulgence. You must hate your soul for the love of Christ; deny and mortify yourself to honor Him and make yourself pleasing and acceptable to Him. If you love and wish to enjoy Him, you must resolve to forget yourself. You must pass through sharp trials before you can see God face-to-face. If you desire Him to dwell in your heart, empty it of yourself and of all creatures.

The Almighty does not wish you to feel lonely and sorrowful out of any ill will He bears you, but because His blessed Son was afflicted, and God would not have us unlike Him. Nothing pleases Him so well as to see in us a resemblance to His only-begotten Son. What so touches the soul as to see our Lord upon the Cross, tortured for the love of us? The more afflicted and deformed by pain He appears, the more beautiful He seems to us; so the more we suffer for Him, the better will His Father love to look on us. Thus, we strive to beautify our souls with the crimson hue of suffering to win God's favor, just as fashionable women suffer pain and take trouble to attract the admiration of men. Our hearts must be changed in order to satisfy God; they must be purified as gold from which the dross is melted by fire before it comes from the crucible bright and glittering. We would be ashamed of our weak efforts to please God, if only we realized the importance of gaining His approval, for we ought to be willing to shed our blood to gain His love.

While pondering over this truth, a holy hermit saw a woman of the world pass by, magnificently dressed and bejeweled. He burst into tears, exclaiming: "I beseech Thee to pardon me, O Lord, for this woman in one day takes more trouble to please men, than I have done in many years to please Thee!"[27]

---

[27] The monk was St. Nonnus, Bishop of Heliopolis, and the woman St. Pelagia, an actress at Antioch, of bad repute, who had formerly been a catechumen. A few days after the incident recorded, she

The love of God does not consist in mere words, but in sorrow and bitter sufferings, in being despised by the world, abandoned by all creatures, and, it may seem, at times, in the withdrawal of even our Creator's favor. In spite of all these trials, the Christian's courage must be firm; he must not complain, nor lose heart; he should imitate the martyr who, while they were disemboweling him and tearing the flesh from his bones with iron hooks, had no word on his lips but the name of Jesus, nor any thought in his heart but "Blessed be God." He was willing and resolute to bear even greater torments, if it pleased God to send them.

Affliction, when borne for Christ, is both a gift and a grace, which He bestows only on His favorites. It is an act of great mercy to let off with a few cuffs a criminal who has been sentenced to a flogging; and if we can expiate the punishment due to us in the next world by suffering here, let us endeavor to satisfy God's justice on earth, so that at our death we may behold His face without delay. Let us lead lives of penance during our exile here, that when we die, we may enter at once into our heavenly country.

St. Augustine says that it wrongs a martyr to pray for him after his death, for martyrdom makes the soul fly straight to Heaven. Let us strive to be martyrs by patience, for although our pains may be less severe, they last longer. We ought not to wish for a happy life, but prefer a martyrdom on earth; it was our Lord's portion, and He wishes ours to be the same. Some have died as martyrs for

---

heard St. Nonnus preach a sermon on the Last Judgment that so touched her heart that she went to him and with many tears begged him to baptize her. He did so, and, giving all her riches to the poor, she went to the Holy Land, where, under the name of Pelagius, she spent many years in penance, shut up in a narrow cell with only a small aperture for a window. She acquired the reputation of a saint, and at her death, the people were surprised to discover that she was not a man: the virgins of the neighborhood bore her body to their church as a rich treasure.

the Faith, and others have gone to Heaven without doing so, but we must all be martyrs of love, if we wish to arrive there.

This love must be a torment and a pain to us, because of the offense given to God by ourselves and others; it must deprive us of all comfort in life and load our shoulders with the cross. It must make us embrace hardships and overcome them by the burning charity God has kindled in us. This love so carries us out of ourselves that it makes us perfectly insensible to dishonor, as wine takes away the reason of a drunkard. Like all strong affection, it makes a man forget himself and care only for his Beloved, who, in this case, is God Himself and His most holy will. Although this affection seems to treat us cruelly now, what mercy will it not gain hereafter for the soul that has been its living martyr! We cannot fully realize the strength of the love that tortures us here and will console us in the next world.

Let us believe what God has told us of it and walk in the faith of His word, for we have still a long journey before us. Whether your afflictions be light but last long, or short and severe, from one or the other you cannot escape. Do not grieve at this, for if God sends you many sufferings, it is because your sins deserve them, and through them you will atone for your faults, as I pray God you may do.

I do not wish you to go to Purgatory after my death, for perhaps there would be no one to take pity on your soul and endeavor to deliver it as I should; if you were to die first, I should have a hard task to set you free.

Pardon my saying so, but it is not right that either you or I should think only of our own interests. Even if we knew we were to be tormented hereafter, we ought, while on earth, to muster strength to suffer out of love, because love needs no reward but itself. Christ died for love of us; let us suffer for love of Him. He carried His Cross: let us help Him to bear it. He was dishonored; therefore, I renounce honor; He suffered torments; let them come to me. He lived wanting many necessaries; let me go destitute. Jesus made Himself a stranger for me; let me have nothing in which my heart can rest. He died for me; may my life be a continual death for the love of Him.

Oh! that I might say, "I live, now not I, but Christ liveth in me"[28]—and that, Christ crucified, agonized, and abandoned by all save God. Behold Christ whom I love! Upon the Cross I seek Him, and away from it I do not wish to find Him! He may do with me what He will; I choose sorrow for my portion for His sake. Let Him decide whether to reward me or not; to suffer for Him is all I ask. The greatest boon I beg from my Savior is to send the suffering, for it will prove my love for Him, and His for me, if He put me on the cross on which He stretched Himself. Although I seek nothing for myself, it is certain if I stay upon the cross, He will bear me to His Kingdom.

To Him be glory, world without end!

---

[28] Gal. 2:20.

7

To a Gentleman

How God Heals Us Through the Grace of Illness

You may well be content to serve our Lord in illness, for when he calls people to *suffer* instead of *working* for Him, He is calling them to a higher state. During our earthly exile, it is most fitting that we should carry the cross with Christ, who loved it so dearly that He chose to die on it. We can do this better in sickness than in health, for illness is repugnant to flesh and blood and can never cause vainglory.

Great were the works of Christ in His mortal life, but greater far were His sufferings, which exceeded those of the whole world. This idea explains St. James's words: "My brethren, count it all joy, when you shall fall into divers temptations"; and again: "Patience hath a perfect work."[29] Receive your illness, then, willingly, and be grateful to our Lord, who sent it. If you bear this cross and burden well, He will send you interior and more painful trials, which He keeps for His dearest friends, to conform them to Himself. For although Christ's visible Cross was great, it was not to be compared with that which, unknown to men, He bore in His soul.

Although you may think that God has taken you away from other work because you performed it badly, thank Him

[29] James 1:2, 4.

nonetheless for doing so. To be corrected by the hand of so loving a Father needs rather humility to restrain our excessive joy, than patience to bear our punishment well. However, I fear lest you may not profit by this sickness as you should, for sometimes beginners become lax in their religious duties when suffering from an illness that is not dangerous to life. How foolish it is to change medicine into poison, and injure our souls with the thing God sends us for a remedy. Call on Him for aid with all your heart, that as He has weakened your body by His touch, your soul may run to Him the more swiftly. This infirmity is sent that your flesh may expiate its sins by suffering pain; so do not turn this chance of discharging your past debts into a time for incurring fresh ones.

Watch carefully over your conduct; do not think your body must have everything it asks for, but by the aid of the Holy Spirit, offer it to Christ crucified, and He who let Himself be placed between two thieves, will not drive you from Him. Although you cannot now keep up your customary reading and meditation as you would wish, still, do all you can without serious injury to your health. Our Lord is so good and so powerful that He gives strength to those He sees to be doing their best. Sometimes He bestows more favors on people who lie ill in bed and are unable to pray than on others who spend hours in prayer. Perhaps He will show you this mercy, which depends solely on His will.

In conclusion, I beg you, for the love of God, not to "be carried about by every wind of doctrine,"[30] but to preserve your high esteem for those persons through whose hands you have received divine mercy. Imitate the man in the Gospel who was born blind: he considered his cure a proof of the goodness of his Master who had worked it and would let no one persuade him to the contrary. He said: "If he be a sinner, I know not: one thing I know, that

---

[30] Eph. 4:14.

whereas I was blind, now I see."[31] Although this man said: "If he be a sinner," evidently he was convinced of our Lord's justice, as is shown by his persistently maintaining it in his answers to the Jews, and also by Christ's making Himself known to him in the Temple as the reward of his faith.

I have heard accusations made against these Jesuit Fathers by people who are jealous of them, but I believe that neither these, nor any other charges that could be brought against them, have any true foundation. I wish you, however, to speak mildly in their defense and with moderation, for God takes such matters under His special protection and wishes them to be borne with patience and sweetness.

I beg our Blessed Lord, who died for you, to remain with you.

---

[31] John 9:25.

8

To a Middle-Aged Couple

How to Save Your Souls

You ask me to give you some advice about saving your soul: a demand most reasonable and worthy to be granted if only my ability were equal to my good will.

When a man first has the use of his reason, he should begin so to regulate his life that when death comes, his days may all have been spent in preparation for worthily receiving the crown of glory. When maturer age, the forerunner of death, arrives, he must repent and make amends for any past negligence. This is the time to renew our courage and to exert ourselves to remedy the weaknesses of our youth and to devote ourselves with fervor to making ready for death.

This preparation consists not only in setting ourselves free from both debts and mortal sin, but in doing penance for our past faults, so that when our good and evil deeds are put into the balance of justice, with the divine mercy added to the right side of the scale, our attachment to God's service may weigh as much as our former attachment to the world. We ought to give alms, to be charitable, devout, patient, and humble, in order to compensate for our former defects in these virtues. Busy like a honey-making bee, with a holy fervor, we should seek to get nearer and nearer to God; for at our time of life, the hour approaches when we shall appear before Him. How shall we answer our Sovereign Judge, if we have spent carelessly those later years He has most mercifully given us, in which to amend the past and prepare ourselves for Heaven? Therefore, care less for temporal things and attend instead to those which are more important.

Withdraw your heart from the world before God takes your body from it: keep your mind in perfect peace however much it is occupied in business. A man who is traveling post haste concerning a matter that is of life and death to him does not turn his head to look at anything as he passes. You must cultivate the same indifference to mundane matters. Say in your heart, "I am being led captive to death; what is this world to me? I am going to God; I do not wish to entangle myself in earthly things." If, in spite of all our efforts, we often find our attention distracted from religious matters, what would it be if we took no pains to be recollected? Consider that you are only beginning to serve God; remember your former good resolutions, and beg God to assist you in carrying them out, for you have more experience as to the best means of keeping them now than you had before.

Your life consists in drawing nearer to God; to do this, you must endeavor to detach yourself from visible things and remember that in a short time they will all be taken from you. Practice spiritual reading and prayer; go to confession and Holy Communion; and let the one object of your life be to serve God and to bear with things contrary to your will. Be most tender in your love for God and your neighbor; act in as charitable a way as possible to others, and be firm as a rock in bearing the trials sent you by Divine Providence. Good works are of no use unless we bear the cross as well, nor do sufferings profit us unless we lead a Christian life. If this seem hard to us, let us contemplate our Lord and Master, and see how many were His labors and pains. What He was, that He wishes His followers to be, each in his own measure, for He asked and obtained from His Father that where He was there might His servants also be. Therefore, we must not fear to follow Him in His pains here below and yet wish to share with Him in His present bliss. Although it be the more painful part to partake of His sorrows, it is the better, for we shall enjoy our Lord's presence more fully for having toiled for Him here. "If we suffer with Him, we shall also reign with Him."[32] Do not let us be incredulous about this promised reward nor slow in trying to gain it, for after a brief time of toil, we shall enjoy eternal happiness.

Kindly consider this letter as written to your wife as well as to yourself. You must help each other and walk together in the right path so as to be companions in Heaven, mutually enjoying the sight of God, for He has "joined you together on earth."

[32] 2 Tim. 2:12.

9

To a Young Jesuit Dying

On Consolations Found in Death

The grace of the Holy Spirit be ever with you.

They tell me you are passing so swiftly on your way to the land of the living, that, even while I write this, you may already be enjoying the embraces of our sweetest Jesus. However, I am sending you my congratulations on your promotion to be prebendary[33] in the heavenly Jerusalem, where God is praised to all eternity and seen face-to-face.

Go on your way, then, dearest Father, in that joyful, and thrice joyful, hour, to the supreme Good, and enjoy Him forever. Depart in that blessed hour, to dwell in the bosom of the celestial Father, where He receives those lambs which He fed with His grace and led with His staff. Then, at last, will you know what a favor our Lord did you in calling you to the religious life, and in giving you the grace to despise the world and to follow Him by the way of the cross, for Heaven will be the reward of your

---

[33] St. John playfully compares the position of a prebendary, who resides within the precincts of a cathedral and constantly attends its services, to that of the saints who "stand before the throne" of God and "rest not day nor night, saying 'Holy, holy, holy, Lord God almighty'" and whose company the dying Jesuit hoped soon to join.

consecration to God's service and glory, and your payment for the cross you bore for Christ's love.

Blessed be our Lord Jesus Christ for His goodness in bestowing such honors on the worms of the earth; "raising up the needy from the dust, that he may sit with princes."[34] Welcome be the hour in which the body dies and the soul ascends to take its seat among the princes who dwell forever in the presence of God. O day that ends all our sorrows and all our sins! O day on which we rise to Heaven and begin to serve God perfectly, without the pain and discouragement we experience here because we can render Him only scant service! Here we halt, and faint, while longing to please God and to give Him all our hearts; but in Heaven this wish is so fully granted, that the whole man is employed in the worship of his Creator without let or impediment.

Glory be to God, who hath gathered you so early into His granary, lest wickedness should alter your understanding, and who will show you His bountiful loving kindness by granting you an eternity of bliss, in return for the few years you have dedicated to Him in this world. Behold, Reverend Father, what a God He is! The reward earned by His grace is the fruit of His Passion; it is our blessed fate to have fallen into the hands of such a Lord, and to know Him, and to love Him, although, alas! with many imperfections. He cleanses us from our faults with His Blood; He gives us His sacraments. His fatherly love grants an easy pardon to our sins and a generous reward for our services. He leads us through the Red Sea to the Promised Land, setting our sins as far apart from us as the East is from the West. He drowns them in His Precious Blood, so that, although we still see them, they are dead, and only incite us to praise our Lord, "Who hath thrown the horse and the rider into the sea."[35] Go, then, with God's blessing, to enjoy and

---

[34] 1 Kings 2:8 (RSV = 1 Sam. 2:8).
[35] Exod. 15:1.

rejoice in the riches of your tender Father, which He gained for you in bitter warfare by the shedding of His Blood, for He never fails to succor those who place their hope and love in Him.

We shall all miss you, dear Father, and feel lonely without you, but as God calls you to this blessed lot, our love for you will make us happy in your gain. For, although we shall grieve at our loss, we shall rejoice for you, as the brothers of Rebecca did, when she left them to be espoused to Isaac, whose name signifies "joy." Therefore we say to you: "Thou art our brother; mayst thou increase to thousands of thousands, and may thy seed possess the gates of their enemies."[36]

It is not for me to counsel you how to prepare for this great festival, for there are those around you who can direct and help you to pass from the hands of men into those of God. May the Savior, who came into the world and was raised upon the cross for you, be your succor, so that, although you walk through the valley of the shadow of death, you may fear no evil. Cry to your Redeemer, for although you should be in the belly of the whale, He can hear you even there. Call upon His Blessed Mother, who is our Mother too; supplicate the saints, who are our fathers and our brethren, for with such aids as these, you need not fear to lose the heavenly kingdom. If our Lord wills you to pass through Purgatory, may His name be blessed, for with the hope of seeing Him, you will welcome its pains.

May Christ, who died for you, be with you at your death and receive your soul into His arms as it leaves this world. Say to Him, as He said to His Father: "Father, into Thy hands I commend my spirit,"[37] and I trust that in His mercy He will receive you as His son, and as the heir of God, and joint heir with Himself in His kingdom of Heaven.

[36] Cf. Gen. 24:60.
[37] Luke 23:46.

10

To Friends Under Threats and Persecution[38]

On the Honor Found in Suffering for Christ

"Blessed be the God and Father of our Lord Jesus Christ, the Father of mercies, and the God of all comfort, who comforteth us in all our tribulation; that we also may be able to comfort them who are in all distress, by the exhortation wherewith we also are exhorted by God. For as the sufferings of Christ abound in us, so also by Christ doth our comfort abound."[39]

These are the words of the apostle St. Paul. Thrice he was scourged with rods, five times with whips, and once he was stoned in such a way that he was left for dead. He was persecuted by men of all conditions, and exposed to all sorts of afflictions and trials, and this so often that he says in another part of his writings: "We who live are always delivered unto death for Jesus' sake: that the life also of Jesus may be made manifest in our mortal flesh."[40] In spite of all these sufferings, he never murmured or complained of the way God treated him, as weak souls do; or gave way to grief, as men do who care for their own honor and comfort; or prayed the Almighty to deliver him from his pains, like those who cannot understand their value and therefore desire to be freed from them.

[38] Possibly the Jesuits of Salamanca.
[39] 2 Cor. 1:3-5.
[40] 2 Cor. 4:11.

Unlike some Christians who shirk sufferings, he does not think them slight graces only. Far from it; rising above all ignorance and weakness, he blesses our Lord during his torments, and gives Him thanks for them as for a signal mercy. The apostle holds himself happy to bear something in honor of Christ, who bore such dishonor to raise us from the base condition in which our sins had placed us. For indeed, our Lord beautified our souls and honored us with the gift of His Spirit, and by adopting us as sons of God, He gave us a pledge that from Him and through Him, we should one day enjoy the kingdom of Heaven.

Oh, my most dear brothers, God seeks to show you what a favor He does us, when the world thinks He punishes us. Oh, what an honor it is for us to be disgraced for seeking God's honor, and what glory we shall one day get for the affronts we suffer now! How merciful, loving, and gracious, are the arms our Lord holds out to receive those who are wounded in the combat for His sake! In this our true joy far exceeds every bitterness the sorrow of this world can give. If we are wise, we shall long for these caresses; for who, that understands true happiness, does not long for what is unmixed love and wholly to be desired? Be sure, that, if you wish for this, and to see and enjoy Heaven, the path of suffering is the safest to lead you there. This is the way that Christ and all His servants trod, and which He calls "the narrow way which leads to life."[41] He taught us, that, if we wish to come to Him, we must follow Him, for it is not right that the Son of God should have endured dishonor, and the sons of men should pass through life without it. "For the disciple is not above his Master nor the servant above his Lord."[42] God forbid that our souls should find rest in or choose any other lot but that of suffering beneath our Lord's Cross. I know not if bearing the cross can be called "pain," for to my mind it is to repose on a bed of down and roses.

[41] Cf. Matt. 7:14.
[42] Matt. 10:24.

O Jesus of Nazareth! — the name signifying "a flower" — how sweet is Your odor, which wakes in us desires of eternity, making us forget our sorrows, at the thought of Him for whom we bear them and of the reward He will bestow on us for doing so. Who that loves You does not love You *crucified*? In that Cross, You both sought and found me, cured and made me free, and, loving me, gave Your life-blood for me, by the hands of cruel wretches!

Therefore, on Your Cross I seek You; there do I find You, and You heal me and deliver me from myself — me, who only obstructs Your love for me, which is my salvation. Now, delivered from my self-love, which is Your enemy, I give You my love, which, although not equal to, is at least some poor imitation of the excessive love You showed upon the Cross for me, in that, loving You, I suffer for You, as You, for love, died for me! But alas, what shame and sorrow must I feel! The many torments You bore for me witness to the greatness of Your love, and yet I show how tepidly I love You in return, by the little I endure for Your sake.

Well do I know that there are few who deserve the great happiness of being marked as Your own with the seal of the cross; yet think how sad it is for me to desire, and not to obtain, to ask and not to receive, especially when what I ask for is not *joy*, but *afflictions* for Your sake! Tell me, why will You have me both for Your herald and Your ensign-bearer to carry the standard of Your gospel, and yet will not permit me to wear Your uniform? How ill it looks that I should be in the ranks of those who serve You and yet not wear that garment with which You were so constantly, so willingly, and so entirely clothed! Tell us, O beloved Jesus, by Your sweetest Cross, was there a single day on which You put off Your robe of suffering, to wrap Yourself in rest? Or did You ever put off that white garment which so wore its way to Your very Heart, that You did say: "My soul is sorrowful even unto death"?[43]

---

[43] Matt. 26:38.

Ah no! You never did rest, for You never ceased to love us and therefore to suffer for us! When they stripped You of Your robe, they cut out for You upon the Cross, as upon a table, a cloak so long that it clothed You from head to foot, covering Your body and hands, so that there was no part of You that was not dyed with Your most precious blood, and made crimson, and resplendent, and priceless. Your blood flowed from Your head with the thorns, from Your face with the blows, from Your hands with the nails, from Your feet with another nail (most cruel indeed to You, but most precious to us), and from Your whole body with stripes that could hardly be numbered. He who, looking on You, loves himself and not You does You great wrong. If, when the soul sees You in such a plight, it flies from the sufferings that would make it resemble You, its love for You is imperfect, for it does not wish to be made like to You; therefore, it has but little desire to suffer for You. He who loves You with perfect love dies to self for love of You crucified and is more eager to be disgraced for Your sake than to receive all the honors that this world, which is both deceived and a deceiver, can give him.

Let all things be accounted as nothing in comparison with Your Cross — all that flourishes on earth and so quickly fades. Let worldlings blush for shame, for You have fought them at such bitter costs to Yourself and have conquered by Your Cross. Let those who are counted among Your servants be abashed at not rejoicing at the world's antagonism to them, since You were reproached and abandoned and contradicted by it, blind as it is, for it neither sees nor can see that You are the Truth. But I will hold fast to You, even though all other things fail me, for anything else is but misery and mere nothingness; I will wear no livery but Yours, even though it would secure the whole world for me. For to own all which is not You is but a burden and affliction rather than riches, but to possess You, and be possessed by You, is joy to the heart and true riches, for You are the one true Good.

I have forgotten, my dear brothers, that I commenced by begging and admonishing you in Christ's name not to be distressed or surprised at the persecutions, or rather the shadow of them, raised against us, as if they were strange or unusual for God's servants. For this is nothing but the proof, or examination of the lesson we have been learning for the last five or six years, which is "to suffer — to suffer for the love of Christ." Now that it has come upon us, do not let it frighten us; do not let us be like children who will not repeat the lesson they have learned, but be strengthened in the Lord and in the power of His might. He will defend you for love of you, and although He is but one, He is more powerful than all the rest together, being omnipotent. Do not fear that He lacks wisdom, for He knows all things; and no one need fear being disturbed who is held fast to God by the three strong bonds of infinite love, power, and wisdom.

Care nothing for the menaces of your persecutors. As for myself, I tell you truly that their threats do not weigh a hair's weight with me, for I am entirely in the hands of Christ. I deeply pity their blindness, for the gospel that I preached in their town is hidden from their sight. As St. Paul says: "The god of this world, which is the devil, hath blinded the minds of unbelievers, that the light of the gospel of the glory of Christ should not shine upon them."[44]

I earnestly desire and beg of God to be merciful to them and give them blessings, in return for the curses they have heaped on others, and to give them glory for their insults, or rather, what they have sought to do to me, for I hold that, in reality, the only true honor in this world is to be dishonored for Christ's sake.

Act in the same way, dear friends, and be followers of Him who gave to the man who had sold Him to His enemies the kiss of peace and the name of friend, and who cried out on the Cross:

[44] 2 Cor. 4:4.

"Father, forgive them, for they know not what they do."[45] Look upon all your fellowmen as God's creatures, whom He desires to be saved, and you will find that you cannot wish harm to those for whom God has such good will. Remember how often I have told you we must love our enemies, and keep our heart at peace, speaking ill of no man. Be patient in this time of trial, for our Lord will soon bring about a change of circumstances. On no account desist from any good work you have commenced, for that would be most wrong. Be thoroughly convinced that He whom you have followed is the Lord of heaven and earth, of life and of death, and that, in fine, even though all the world should strive to prevent it, His truth must prevail. Endeavor to follow Him, and then you need fear neither men nor devils nor even the angels, if it were possible for them to be against you in this.

Speak little with men, but much with God in prayer in the depths of your heart, for all good must come to us from Him. He wishes us to obtain it through prayer, and especially to keep before our minds the Passion of Jesus Christ our Lord. If you suffer anything by the tongues of wicked men (and that is the only injury they can do you), take it as a satisfaction for your sins, and a special mercy from Christ. He uses them like a cloth to cleanse you from your faults, for *they* will be defiled by the foul things they say, while *you* will be purified by suffering, and your happiness in the next world made sure.

I would however, on no account, have you think yourself any better than those whom you see now in error, for you do not know how long you may continue in the right path, nor how soon they may amend. Work out your salvation in fear and humility, and hope to reach heaven yourselves without thinking that your neighbor will never get there. Acknowledge the Almighty's mercies to you, without reflecting on other people's shortcomings,

---

[45] Luke 23:34.

for you know that the history of the Pharisee and the Publican is intended for a warning to us.

No sanctity is secure without the holy fear of God, in which I would have you "grow old,"[46] as the Holy Scriptures say, by which they mean to teach us that we must not only begin with this fear, but persevere in it to the end. This fear is not irksome, but pleasant, and rids the heart of all levity: it keeps a man from self-confidence in his own merits, however good his actions may be, so that he leaves God to be the Judge both of himself and and of his neighbor, as St. Paul says: "Neither do I judge my own self, but he that judgeth me is the Lord." This is He whom you must fear if you would continue in the right way, so that what you build up may not fall, but stand firmly and rise upward until it reaches the most high God; which end is to be accomplished by love.

I pray our Lord Jesus Christ to bestow this love on you. Amen.

Pray fervently for me, as I believe you do, and I hope that He will hear you and allow me to continue serving you as in former times.

[46] Ecclus. 2:6.

11

To a Grieving Mother

Why Suffering Well Is More
Pleasing to God Than Mere Gratitude

Madam,

I think that you must be feeling grief: much, however, as I desire your happiness, your spiritual progress is more to me, so that I would rather see you bearing trials with patience than enjoying peace and devotion. God is better pleased with submission in suffering than with gratitude in prosperity. Remember our Lady's sorrows; during the Passion alone, at the heart-rending sight of her Son being led to execution as a malefactor, bearing a heavy cross on His shoulders, and so altered that she scarcely recognized Him, she suffered more than has been borne by all the mothers in the world at being parted from their children. Think what must have been her woe as she saw Him whom she loved more dearly than herself pass thus from life! What must she have felt, as she held Him, who was both the Son of God and her own child, dead in her arms, when all His cruel torments were ended! And then again, after Christ's Resurrection and Ascension into heaven, when she was separated long years from Him, she felt His absence more keenly than other mothers feel separation from their sons, for her affection was greater than any they can have.

If we glory in being our Lady's servants, should we not share in her dolors? As we gaze on her standing at the foot of our Lord's Cross, let us contemplate her with a soul filled, as hers was, with sorrow, for mourners cannot talk with the lighthearted. So let those who wish for union with the Blessed Virgin and her Son desire some share in their sufferings. When in this world were afflictions ever wanting to this Mother and Son? Was not sorrow always mingled with any joy that they had? Their life was but a painful exile and a heavy cross; until they left this world, they experienced only trouble. At last they are at peace, but even now they do not wish their followers to think of that, but of the trials they bore while living here below.

Our repose is being kept for the future, and it will indeed be sweet. Here let us work manfully. Our Lord has many ready to share His table but few to partake of His sorrows, and it is for us to be among those few, if we would be in the number of His friends. Let us help Him to drink His chalice, for that will show that we love Him sincerely. It is no easy matter to be the friend of Jesus Christ. Suffering borne for Him is the only sure way to test which is the true and which the false friend. Although the draught may be bitter, drink it — think for whom you take it; how soon its taste will pass away; what a reward it will bring you, and it will taste so sweet that you will complain that there is so little given to you.

Learn to love God as He loves you, and know that a true love will make you give yourself wholly to Him, and keep back nothing for yourself. Do not fear to place yourself in God's hands, abandoning yourself entirely to Him, for all that He holds is safe, and all else will certainly be lost. Our Savior has said: "He that loveth his life shall lose it, and he that hateth his life shall keep it."[47] Do not care for the present, as many have done, only to find themselves deceived at last; but lift your eyes to Heaven, for

[47] John 12:25.

which you were created, and pray that you may get there, be the cost what it may. None of those who are already there have passed through the world without greater afflictions than you have; if some of them had less to bear, their tortures were incomparably more severe in Purgatory, for our Lord has ordained that none shall take part in His joys but they who have shared His pains. He has kept this rule with all souls beloved by Him; therefore, let us not complain of it nor feel aggrieved, even if we had the option of passing through life without sharing in the pains He and His Mother bore.

This is the road to Heaven; let us walk in it. It is the Purgatory of our sins; do not let us think it too hard. This is what God's friends must pass through; let those who will spend their time in pleasure. Our Lord told us, knowing well what was to come: "Amen, Amen, I say to you, that you shall lament and weep, but the world shall rejoice: and you shall be made sorrowful, but your sorrow shall be turned into joy. A woman, when she is in labor, hath sorrow, because her hour is come: but when she hath brought forth the child, she remembereth no more the anguish, for joy that a man is born into the world. So also you now indeed have sorrow, but I will see you again and your heart shall rejoice."[48] These are our Lord's words, and for the sake of the joys to come, forget your present pains, and wait patiently until you see our Lord, who will come sooner than you expect Him.

---

[48] John 16:20-23.

12

To a Friend in the World

*Why Our Resolutions Must Be
Tested at Home and in the Workplace*

I consider that it is by God's special providence that it has fallen to your lot to have to bear with the person about whom you wrote to me. You have long known that you would have to suffer a great deal in every way, both great and small; and how else could this be accomplished? Besides, how is it possible to learn patience, mortification, and humility, except in trials of a kind such as come from this person and from other members of your household? For although you may have made plenty of good resolutions to bear with others and mortify yourself, unless someone puts them to the test, they are dreams rather than realities. Valor must be shown in battle, or else it is but idle boasting. This seems to be the case with you, for when anything of the sort happens, you are disturbed and behave as badly as the person you are correcting. Patience must be kept at all times, and nothing is to be gained by avoiding the occasions of practicing it. Your outward behavior may be correct when you have nothing to try you, but if the root of the evil is within you, appearances are of no value.

God brings you into contact with people of the kind you mention so that you may master or control your great impetuosity. Be like that youth who, when he was insulted by an old man of

Athens, laughed, saying that he was giving him for nothing what he had been obliged to pay other men dearly to offer him.[49]

Meditate constantly on the insults our Savior met with, until you are able to rejoice at receiving the same treatment; consider yourself fortunate when you meet with it, as it enables you to please our Lord. St. Elizabeth,[50] the daughter of the King of Hungary, was deeply wronged by a large number of people, and she prayed for them with many tears, begging our Lord to bestow some grace on them in return for each injury they had done her. Christ answered her that no petition had ever been so acceptable to Him, and that He pardoned all her sins in return for it.

It is difficult for a man to conquer himself, and especially in his inclinations. It is no small thing in God's eyes to bear being despised by our dependents. This happened to Job, whose servant would neither come, nor pay heed to his master when called by him. Our Redeemer was betrayed by His disciple and received death and dishonor at the hands of those who should have served Him. St. Augustine says: "Do not think that the wicked live in vain, for God keeps them here and suffers them patiently, either

---

[49] This tale is to be found in the *Lives of the Fathers of the Desert*, where it is told by St. John the Dwarf. A philosopher whose disciple had offended him condemned the culprit to carry other people's burdens for three years and then, for the same period, to pay men to insult and annoy him. At the end of that time, the philosopher had his pupil enter the city of Athens to learn wisdom. At the gate sat a wise old man whose custom it was to insult those who entered, out of a desire to learn their dispositions. Our youth laughed at his rudeness and, upon the elder's inquiring the reason, replied: "No wonder, for you have given me gratis what I have had to buy dearly for three years." Upon this, the old man exclaimed: "Enter the city, for you are worthy of it" (see Rosweyde's *Vitæ Patrum*, Bk. III, 84).

[50] St. Elizabeth of Hungary (1207-1231), daughter of King Andreas II of Hungary, niece of St. Hedwig, and widow who became a third-order Franciscan.

that they may be converted, or that they may exercise the virtues of good men." There would have been no Abel without Cain's malice, nor would there have been martyrs, if there had been no cruel executioners. Chastity is not proved unless it is assaulted, nor patience without ill-treatment. Therefore, receive this trial from the hand of God as a very special favor: thank Him for it, and make such good use of it that, with holy Job, who said he would not be without it, you may say: "I was the brother of dragons, and the companion of ostriches."[51]

You will see more dearly how far you have advanced in holiness by the manner in which you bear this trial than you could possibly do while enjoying the sweetness of consolations, or even while suffering illness. For such annoyances as you meet with are so very hard to endure that God is much pleased to find we love Him well enough to bear them well for His sake. This must be the object of all your efforts.

When you have to inflict any punishment, beware of doing so while you feel angry; let the matter rest for the time being, and afterward, from a motive of charity, correct the offender. Use persuasion rather than reproof, for it is a far more efficacious way of benefiting anyone, and this should be our aim in dealing with the faulty, rather than to obtain personal satisfaction for the injury or insult offered to us.

Learn to feign, sometimes, not to see things. Although you may think that discipline is then kept more slackly than well, overlook the offense, for sometimes it is from a secret motive of pride or anger that we are anxious that our servants should behave as they ought toward us.

The heart of man is deep and often deceives itself. Therefore, we should always prefer to mortify ourselves and exercise ourselves by putting up with one offense and then with another,

---

[51] Job 30:29.

until at last, as I have said, when annoyances come, we are actually glad of them and receive them as a boon.

Therefore, it will often be best to take no notice of offenses. As one of my companions, who also possesses a very hasty temper, is accustomed to say: "Behave as if you were deaf and dumb. If you are forced to find fault with anyone, do so gently. Say: 'You know that I desire your good: it pains me to see that you are not what I could wish, nor what our Lord would have you. I am more grieved on this account than at the faults you have committed against me.'"

Thus, be gentle in your correction, and if this is not sufficient, it would be better to inflict some punishment such as fasting, or something else of the kind, than to strike the offender with a stick, or with your hand. If he is incorrigible, you must keep your temper and have him thrashed, and in the meantime, you must pray constantly for him, for nothing can be done without that.[52] Unless you understand that to have servants is to have as many masters, and that you must suffer from them and pray for them, you know nothing of your duty in the matter, nor do you imitate our Lord and the way He treated His disciples. How kind and loving and long-suffering He was with them! He prayed for them and died for them! This is how the superior must behave to his inferiors. Christ showed us this when He washed the Apostles' feet and said: "I have given you an example."[53] In short, behave toward your household more like a father, and a loving father, than with the strictness of a master. Be most gentle and patient and prayerful, and if you show any severity, let it be very slight.

[52] St. Teresa tells us that slavery still existed in Spain, although her father would not allow it in his household. The culprit spoken of in this letter was probably a slave, which accounts for the severity of the corporal punishment that might be necessary, and for the fact that his dismissal is not suggested.

[53] John 13:15.

13

To a Friend

On the Dangers of Spiritual Indecision

Your letter gave me mingled feelings of joy and sorrow; for while I rejoice to hear that you are enjoying better health, I regret to hear that you have grown tepid in your religious duties. Let us thank our merciful Savior for restoring your body, and confess with sorrow the faults we have committed.

Oh, tepidity! If those who give way to it only rightly understood what it is, they would less easily fall victims to it, for they would dread to become the slaves of so cruel a tyrant. If we are free from this vice, nothing we can do or suffer for God, even death itself, seems too great a burden, whereas the victim of tepidity finds a straw too heavy for him to carry. This vice ruins a man's spiritual life, and it not only stops all perseverance in the good he had commenced, but even causes him to repent of having begun it, thus turning into bitterness what should be sweeter than honey to his soul.

The Israelites who journeyed through the desert had appetites so disordered that they could not enjoy the manna "containing in itself all sweetness,"[54] which God sent them. Their blindness was so great that they did not find fault with themselves, or with the

---

[54] Cf. Wisd. 16:20.

evil condition of their health, but with the food, which was of the most savory kind. They asked for some other sort of viand with which they thought they would be better satisfied and pleased; it was given them, but at the cost of their lives. We are to learn by this that even if the things of God are not always agreeable to us, still we must not wish for what is contrary to them, however delightful it may seem to us, for without doubt, it would poison our souls. We should rather rid ourselves of the disgust we feel for religion, and then, when the appetites of our soul are healthy, we shall feel a right and pleasant relish for the food God gives His children.

To work slothfully and tepidly in God's service will cause you to lead so unhappy a life that you will be forced to change your ways. Besides, such a life is disloyal to our Savior, who labored with such ardent love to redeem us and who so willingly took up the Cross that His love for us exceeded His suffering. The tepid soul cannot enjoy the world's pleasures, having given them up in the desire of doing right, and yet, for want of fervor, it does not find happiness in God. In this way, such a soul is placed between two opposites, each of which is a torment to it; it suffers such severe afflictions that at last it leaves the right road and, with miserable fatuity, seeks the flesh-pots of the Egypt it had left, because it cannot endure the hardships of the desert.[55]

Compare the trouble that is undergone by one who serves God diligently and fervently, with that which the tepid soul suffers through sloth, and you will find that the burden borne by tepidity is a thousand times the heavier. It is indeed wonderful that vigils, prayer, fasting, mortification, and other works undertaken for our Lord should bring more pleasure to fervent souls than the tepid find in all their feasts and riches and other indulgences. The luke-warm Christian appears glad, but grief gnaws at his heart, while

[55] Cf. Exod. 16:3.

the just man, even though his life be one of penance, has happiness within his soul.

Why, then, for the sake of shirking a few hardships, do we undergo others far more severe? We prefer dying of hunger to working for our bread. Why cannot we understand that God will reward our labors, and that this reward cannot be earned by boasting of our piety, nor by sleeping or sitting still with folded arms? We should be ashamed to talk of our love for God and at the same time be mean enough to refuse to give ourselves any trouble in His service. Is that to honor God, and to esteem Him? It is not fitting that the soul which values it so cheaply should receive so great a boon.

This is but justice, as our Savior teaches, when He bids us watch and be ready to open when He knocks, like servants waiting for their master. He has said that unless a man takes up his cross and follows Him, he is not worthy of Him. It is not the slothful who take up the cross, but those who love our Lord, who died upon it. It is not they who imitate His courage and will so share in His victory; for the lukewarm begin the work today and slacken in their efforts tomorrow, until by degrees they desist from it entirely. God threatens us with this when He says: "Because thou art lukewarm, I will vomit thee out of my mouth,"[56] which means that He will permit the offender to fall into still graver and fouler sins.

We must not travel on this dangerous road with our eyes shut, for it is full of thieves who would rob and murder us, and there are many pitfalls into which we might slip, and great impediments to be overcome. We have sometimes seen the prudent and cautious in danger; what, then, can we expect, if we are careless, except that at every chance we should fall as miserable captives into the hands of our enemies?

[56] Cf. Apoc. 3:16 (RSV = Rev. 3:16).

Let us, then, be diligent, whether it be from motives of fear or of love, and not permit tepidity to master us, for, like gall, it not only embitters religion to us, but it makes our service distasteful to God. Let us set to work in earnest, for, as the Holy Scripture says: "If thou be diligent, thy harvest shall come as a fountain."[57] Then we shall experience the truth of Christ's promise that He would give to those who serve Him a water, of which he who drinks shall never more be thirsty. If He gives this water to us during this life, what will He not give to us in the world to come? If such solace is given us during the battle, what shall be the feast of victory? Let us do violence to ourselves, for that is the way to come to the kingdom; and in proportion as we deny ourselves and renounce our inclinations do we advance on our way to Heaven and become more pleasing to God.

I do not think you should employ yourself in study until you have spent at least a year, and more if necessary, in eradicating from your heart all its evil habits and propensities. You should set about this at once, for until it is done, I consider that you ought to attend to nothing else.

[57] Prov. 6:11.

14

To a Lady

On Scruples and Spiritual Cowardice

It is very plain, my dear sister, that you cannot bear being put to the test, nor have you yet emerged from spiritual childhood, for when your heavenly Bridegroom ceases to smile on you, you immediately imagine He is displeased with you. Where are the signal favors you received from His blessed hand as a pledge of His special love for you? Ought you so soon to forget how He has cherished you or to believe that God would lightly withdraw affection He bestowed so fully? Why did He grant so many proofs of it, if not to make you trust Him? Be assured that He loves you, even if He does not show it at the present moment.

You need not fear deception on this point, for, as I have often told you, our love for God should not cause us excessive sadness whenever we commit some venial sin. If this were necessary, who would ever be at rest or peace, for we are all sinners? May our Lord give you grace to lean on Him and rejoice in Him, placing your wounds in His, that you may be healed and comforted, however violent and painful your hurt may be.

How long will you continue your minute self-examinations? It is like raking up a dust heap from which nothing can come but rubbish and unpleasantness. Feel sure of this, that it is not for your own merits, but for those of Jesus crucified, that you are loved and made whole. Do not give way to such discouragement about your faults; the results will show you how displeasing it is to God. It would be far better to be courageous and strong-hearted. Meditate on the benefits you have received through Jesus Christ in the past and possess now; reflect on them in such a manner as to lead you to sorrow for your sins against Him and to avoid offending Him, without losing your peace and patience if you happen to fall. As I have often repeated, God loves you as you are. Be content that His love should come from His goodness, and not from your merits. What does it matter to a bride if she is not beautiful, if the bridegroom's affection for her makes her seem so in his eyes? If you look only on yourself, you will loathe yourself and your many defects will take away all your courage.

What more have you to wish for? In Heaven there is One to whom you appear all fair, for He looks at you through the apertures of the wounds He received for you; by these He gives you grace and supplies what is lacking in you, healing you and making you lovely. Be at peace: you are indeed the handmaid of the crucified Christ. Forget your past misdoings as if they had never been. I tell you, in God's name, as I have done before, that such is His holy will.

Run swiftly on your way with a light foot, like one who has thrown off his shoulders a heavy burden that hindered his course. If the longed-for quiet does not come at once, do not distress yourself; sometimes one travels farther in a storm than in a calm, and war gains more merits than peace. He who redeemed you will guide you aright so that you may be safe. Trust in Him; He has given you many reasons to do so; and when you consider your own defects, consider also the depths of His mercy, which will help you far more than thinking about your deficiencies.

May God's mercy shelter you beneath His everlasting love, as I desire and pray and trust that it may, and for this I bid you hope. Recommend me to the same Lord for the sake of His love.

15

To a Friend

On the First Steps to Holiness

I have received your letters, and although I do not answer them all, do not cease to ask me whatever you wish to know, if you really desire to be as holy as you say. A contrary course of action would be neither humble nor obedient, and therefore, not the way of the saints.

The first thing by which to attain great sanctity is to consider that you are wicked and that God is infinitely good, and that it is only by His graces that sinners are made good Christians, and that good Christians become better still.

You must be most loyal to our Lord Jesus Christ by giving Him the glory for any virtues you possess. This is the matter, above all others, on which He is susceptible to injustice, and He leaves those who defraud Him of these His claims without honor or graces. You must also love Him fervently, if you would be perfect, for holiness comes from love, and the greater the love, the greater the saint. The best proof we can give of our love for Christ is to obey His commands and bear the cross for Him; the greater the modifications and hardships this entails, the more does it bear witness to the genuineness of our love.

Contempt for self and abnegation of our will are also signs of this love, for our Lord says: "If any man will come after me, let him deny himself."[58] A truly devout soul is at enmity with its own judgment and self-will, and is grateful when it receives insults or annoyances, as they give it the opportunity of conquering these vices. Until a man has obtained from God this self-hatred, so that he takes vengeance on himself by penance as far as possible and is glad that other men should avenge Christ's cause on him, he has not traveled far on the way of that perfect love of our Lord which causes the soul to have a holy hatred toward self, so that it may have a true love of God and of itself.

Another outcome of deep love of our Lord is a perfect charity toward our neighbor, which grows as our love for God increases, making its possessor as much at one with his brethren, as if they were members of the same body; it moves him to pray fervently for others and do penance for their welfare when it is possible. May your heart forever be wholly given to Christ.

[58] Matt. 16:24.

16

To a Wealthy Lady

On Acquiring the Love of God

Madam,

It is a great pleasure to hear of your holy desire to serve God, but I regret your want of courage in putting it into execution. It is extremely wrong for anyone to dare to continue living in a worldly manner, and not begin to live for God, confiding in His help. My dear sister, since the human race existed, has any man who trusted in his Creator, and obeyed His commands, ever been abandoned by Him? Has anyone persevered in calling on God with his whole heart, and not been heard? Nay, rather, the Almighty is always seeking us and urging us to serve Him. If we draw near to Him, what can He, who is so good and so faithful to His promises, do but come forth to meet and embrace us, and give us His help and protection? Yes, most truly and most certainly He will, as St. Paul tells us, far more fully than we can possibly imagine. Begin, then, servant of God, begin: cast yourself upon Him, and be confident that He, who inspired you with the desire will give you strength to carry it out and perfect it to the end. Our Lord does not arouse one who sleeps, except to give him many favors on his awaking.

Take courage, and set out with diligence and fervor: nothing is worse than for a beginner to commence badly by indulging his body and trying to please the world. Shut your ears against all human praise or blame, for in a little while, both the critic and the man he judges will be dust and ashes. We shall one day stand before God's tribunal, where the mouth of wickedness shall be stopped and virtue will be exalted. Meanwhile, embrace the cross, and follow Him who was dishonored and who lost His life upon it for your sake. Hide yourself in our Lord's wounds, so that when He comes, He may find you dwelling in Himself. Then He will beautify you with His graces and give Himself to you as your reward for having left all things, even yourself, for His sake.

How little, indeed, does the man who forsakes all things give up! He but leaves now, what, whether he will or not, he can keep but for a very brief time. Even while he possesses it, it brings him misery, for all that is not God only burdens and saddens the soul, which its Creator alone can satisfy. Open your heart to Him, and rejoice in Him, and you will find Him more tender and loving than can be imagined.

I sometimes wonder how anyone can possibly wish evil to others, for our Lord stands between him and them. How can he be harsh toward the body, who loves, or ought to love, the Head? Do you not know, my dear sister, that when Jesus rose again and appeared to His disciples, He placed Himself "in the midst of them," and not at the head or elsewhere? He acted thus to show that He is in the midst of us and that we cannot wish harm, nor do wrong to anyone, without first doing it to Him. The person who wishes evil to his neighbor, wishes evil to Christ, and it would be better for that man never to have been born, since he ignores that the end for which he was created was to love our Lord. You should realize that your neighbors are very dear to Christ, that they are created in His image and that He gave His blood for them. Say to yourself, then, "How can I wish ill to those to whom my Lord wishes well? How can I desire death to those to whom He desires to give life? Jesus died for these souls, and would do so again if there were need, and shall not I love those who are so dear to Him? What does it matter if they injure me? I do not love them because of what they are, nor for the way they treat me, but for Christ's sake alone. Why should their evil deeds destroy the affection I bear them on His account? I ask of God that they may be acceptable to Him, that they may please Him, and enjoy His favor, so that there may be more temples in which He may dwell; more souls to praise Him and more hearts to love Him as He deserves."

Offer up this prayer: "O Lord, take possession of these souls and make them wholly Yours; may they enjoy Your presence within them, for You are ready to give Yourself to all. O my God, they are created in Your image; make them resemble You more and more, and grant, both to them and to us all, pardon, grace, and glory." If your nature rebels against this prayer, utter it in spirit and lift up your heart to Christ, crying: "For Your loving sake, O Lord, and not for their merits"; and so, little by little, you will find yourself in peace. If you should have to struggle with yourself, still do not let yourself be overcome; neither say nor do anything uncharitable, nor let your heart consent to any unkind thought about others.

Your scruples about confession are temptations by which the Devil tries to deprive you of spiritual joy and rob you of your pleasure in the things of God. A scrupulous soul is not fit to trust or to love God and, as it does not find what satisfies it in Him, is not contented with the way by which He leads it and forsakes Him to seek its happiness elsewhere; it commits the fatal error of raising a storm where there was a calm. It follows its own conceits, and not God's way, which is always sweet and simple. Treat your anxieties as a jest; obey your confessor's advice; do not give way to your own judgment. You must not allow your scruples to influence you, but say "God is not scrupulous. I do what is commanded me in His holy name, and that is all I have to answer for." Lose no time in acquiring the love of God, my dear sister, and you will soon get rid of scruples, which spring from a timorous heart, for "perfect love casteth out fear."[59] Cry to our Lord: "*Deus meus illumina tenebras meas:* O my God, enlighten my darkness," and trust to His merciful goodness, that while you serve Him, He will deign to give you more grace to see your faults and amend them. As for your thoughts of vainglory, laugh at them too, and say to them, "I am not doing this action on your account, nor will I cease doing it because of you.[60] O my God, it is to You I offer all that I do, all that I say, all that I think!" When the temptation returns, say: "You have come too late; the work is already given to God."

It is more discreet for beginners not to perform any remarkable exterior acts of piety; their spiritual life is young and tender, and, as it were, only in the bud, and is easily injured by the breath of praise, so it is best for them to hide their graces. Follow this advice when you can, but when it is impossible and your good works must necessarily be seen by others, act with liberty and without fear. When you commence an action, lift up your heart to our Lord, saying: "*Non nobis, Domine, non nobis, sed nomini Tuo da gloriam:* Not unto us, O Lord, not unto us, but to Thy name give glory."[61] Or else "*Gloria Patri et Filio et Spiritui Sancto.*"

In conclusion, I would urge you to cast out of your heart all but God; let your eyes be ever toward Him, that He "may pluck your feet from the snare."[62] Care for nothing in this world but contrition, solitude, humility, and penance. Follow God's law, and you will find how He will make your path straight and cast

---

[59] Cf. 1 John 4:18.

[60] This is an allusion to the well-known tale of St. Bernard, who, when preaching, was tempted by the Devil to be vain of his eloquence and its effects. He said: "I did not begin for you, and I shall not leave off for you," and continued his sermon.

[61] Ps. 113:9 (RSV = Ps. 115:1).

[62] Ps. 24:15 (RSV = Ps. 25:15).

your enemies under your feet. Practice will show you what you could never be taught by word of mouth. Those who are tepid and talkative learn little of God's ways, while others who labor fervently for Him come to know Him well. Our Lord Jesus Christ goes on before you, follow Him with your cross, and one day you will come to be with Him in Heaven.

17

To a Friend

On True Confidence in God

Your Grace,

May the peace of our Lord Jesus Christ be ever with you. If we would not offend God, there are two points on which we must be particularly careful: one is that we should love His goodness, and the second is that we should trust in His mercy. How great is the blindness of a heart that does not love God! And just as great is its weakness, if it does not confide in His abundant mercy. The graces we have received from Him in the past ought to incite us to love Him, for they flowed from divine love, which requires a like return from us.

These gifts ought also to encourage us to trust in God, for surely, He who has already bestowed such benefits on us, and has set us in the path of holiness, will give us the grace to persevere. We ought also to find motives for hope in Christ's Passion: we should love Him for dying for us and trust in His mercy. Cast away, then, all doubts, faintheartedness, and misgivings, for the merits of the Passion are ours, because Christ gave them to us, and we are His.

It is in the Passion that I trust, on it I rely, and by it I laugh my enemies to scorn. Through it I make my prayers to the Father and offer Him His Son; I pay all my debts from Christ's merits, and have more than is requisite for the purpose. Although I have many sorrows, I find in Christ's sufferings more than a sufficient solace; they are such a source of joy that the grief caused by my own defects is dispelled.

O God most loving, who are love itself; how we wound You if we trust not in You with all our hearts! If, after the favors You have shown us, and more than all, after You have died for us, we do not feel confidence in You, we must be worse than the very brutes. After all You have given us in the past, can we doubt Your loving kindness in the future, or think that You will cease to protect those You have saved from Hell? Will You leave Your adopted sons to die of hunger or cease to guide them aright in the path in which You set them when they had wandered away? When we were estranged from You, You gave us many graces; will You then refuse them now when our only desire is to serve You? While we offended against You, You cherished us; You followed after us when we fled from You; You drew us to Yourself, cleansed us from our guilt, and giving to us Your Holy Spirit, filled our souls with joy and bestowed on us the kiss of peace.

And wherefore did You do all this? Surely it was so that we might believe that, as for Christ's sake You reconciled us to Yourself when we were among Your enemies, much more surely will You keep us for His sake, now that we are in the number of Your friends.

O my God and my Mercy! after the countless favors You have shown us, permit not that we distrust You and question whether You love us and intend to save us. More evident than the sun at midday is the witness borne by Your works that You cherish us and give us the hope of salvation.

Let our hearts rely confidently on God, even though we feel not the sweetness of His consolations. Genuine faith believes, without the need of argument or miracles; and love trusts its

Beloved, even though He chastises it; true patience is content to suffer without relief; and so a real confidence in God remains unshaken by the absence of any solace from Him. Let us not ask for any signs of God's favor, but obey His command to rely implicitly on Him, and all will be well with us. If we feel weak, let us rely on God, and we shall be strong: for those who confide in Him "shall take wings as eagles and not faint."[63] If we know not what to do, let us trust in our Creator, and He will be our Light; for, as Isaiah says, "Who is there amongst you that hath walked in darkness and hath no light? Let him hope in the name of the Lord, and lean upon his God."[64] Holy Scripture also tells us: "They that trust in God shall understand the truth."[65]

Let us place our hope in our heavenly Father when we are in trouble, and we shall be set free from it, as David, speaking in His name, says in the Psalms: "Because he hoped in me I will deliver him."[66] These words show that God asks only that we hope in Him, in order that He may deliver us, and this because those who fall in time of tribulation fall because their faith is weak. St. Peter, while he felt no fear, walked on the sea as if it had been dry land; but the instant he lost confidence, he began to sink, and our Lord said to him: "O thou of little faith, why didst thou doubt?"[67] Let us fear lest this reproof should be addressed to us. However wildly the sea of temptations may rage around us, let us go bravely on and not let a thought of fear or mistrust enter our hearts. Rather, let us confide in God's great love for us, which keeps us safe amid all perils.

I have said all this because, as I wish your belief in the Catholic Faith to be pure from all error, and your love for God to be

---

[63] Isa. 40:31.
[64] Isa. 50:10.
[65] Wisd. 3:9.
[66] Ps. 90:14 (RSV = Ps. 91:14).
[67] Matt. 14:31.

without taint of tepidity, so I would have your hope in Him to be free from all distrust and fear. Believe me, God can overcome all our doubts and temptations. May He grant us the grace to be wholly converted to Him and to place all our hope in Him, for if we gave ourselves to our Creator's care, there would be no need of help from creatures. If at times doubts enter our mind, let us put them from us and think of other things, for if God does not give us the means to solve those doubts, we should not trouble ourselves much about them.

I wish you and Don Pedro, to whom this letter is addressed as well as to yourself, to be very discreet in fasting and bodily mortifications during this Lent, but to be careful to practice the advice I have given you. Let your memories observe strict abstinence, not only from all thoughts of created things, but even from thinking of yourselves. Forgetting all things, let us go to God, and abide entirely in Him: let us fast from all consolation in any creature, so that, as our souls dwell in solitude, God may come and fill them, because they are empty of all else. When you place yourself in God's presence, endeavor rather to listen to Him than to speak to Him, and strive more to love Him than to learn from Him.

May the same Jesus Christ, of whom we speak, be with you and with us all. Amen.

18

To a Young Woman

On Trials and Spiritual Abandonment

My dearly loved sister in Christ,

I look upon the special regard for your soul with which God inspires me, as a sign of His favor, for not only does the law of charity require this sympathy from me, but I hope that my compassion for your sorrows will ensure me a share in the joy you are one day to receive from our Lord's hands. May the Almighty be blessed in all things, and may His judgments be adored, for His infinite wisdom knows how to turn to our advantage what seems to us the loss of all things. This He does to teach us our ignorance and insufficiency, so that with full confidence, we may abandon ourselves utterly to His care, trusting that, although we know not how, He will find a remedy for all our ills.

You will have much to struggle against, and your soul will often be perturbed. Your past life will appear to you to merit punishment, and when you think how little you profited by the consolations God sent, you will fear lest they, also, may increase your guilt. Scruples will molest you and make you think yourself to blame for all you suffer. The sadness that afflicts you at the present time, the troubles that beset you on every side, together with the ills you fear in the future, will unite to crush your soul. You will feel like the people of Israel felt, after they had left Egypt, when they found themselves hemmed in by high mountains, with the sea before them, and their enemy in pursuit. Often you will feel like David, when he cried: "I said in the excess of my mind: I am cast away from before thy eyes."[68] The devils will say to you, as they did to him: "There is no salvation for you in your God." You will be brought to such a pass that you will seem to taste the anguish of death, although death itself would appear less horrible, for you will be terrified by a secret dread that God has abandoned you. These trials will make your soul so dry and hard that it will seem as dead and as perverse as that of the wicked in hell. You will cry and not be heard, that in which you sought and hoped to find relief will only make you more disconsolate. God will show you no sign of love, but will seem to turn from you in disdain. These and other trials, which are usually suffered in this affliction, will make you so disgusted with yourself, that you would welcome death as a gain.

What then, ought you to do in such a case? Ought you to give up that hope which Christ has so often bidden you hold fast? Should you give way to that despair to which nature and the temptations of the Devil would lead you? Or ought you not rather to find consolation in the loving kindness of Him who, when He is angry, is mindful of His mercies?

There is no need, my dear sister, for any great deliberation on this subject, but there is much for you to do; there is nothing at which to be dismayed, but great need of courage. Do not feel miserable about the state you are in, but rather, rejoice in God's love for you, although you may not realize it at the time. Do not depend upon your feelings; they are often both misled and deceiving. Neither our confidence in our justification, nor our doubts about it affect the reality. "I do not judge myself," said St. Paul.

---

[68] Ps. 30:23 (RSV = Ps. 31:22).

"He that judgeth me is the Lord."[69] Our folly is so great that it is often best for our souls to think that God loves us but little, or not at all. When we feel dry, sad, despondent, and afflicted, so that we seem to suffer the torments of Hell, our foolishness is more easily kept within bounds than when we are made presumptuous by the freedom and happiness that God's consolations are wont to bring.

Like a loving Father, lest his children fall into negligence and false security, He hides the love He bears them, so that they may always preserve some holy fear to keep them from becoming negligent and so losing the inheritance he is keeping for them in the kingdom of Heaven. God knows how it torments these souls to feel that He is dissatisfied with them, how they are tempted when they think that He turns away from them; yet it is His wish that they should pass through this trial. Watching them and loving them as He does, He dissimulates His tenderness and keeps them safe by teaching them this painful lesson. He is the Father of all mercies, whose love for His children surpasses that of all earthly parents; He alone knows the full meaning of fatherhood, and in comparison with Him, other fathers can hardly be said to love or protect their children; so that He has bidden us call no man on earth our father but Him, our only refuge. So strong is His affection, and so watchful His care for our needs, that His paternity cannot be described in words. Yet this Father, ever anxious for our good, allows us to suffer persecutions from the Devil and from other sources, and not only watches in silence, but Himself sends us more trials and temptations.

After some great sorrow, God usually grants us happiness, as to Abraham He gave "Isaac, the desired," whose name signifies "laughter." After a while, the Almighty plunged the patriarch into grief again by commanding him to kill the son He had bestowed for his consolation. So does God often deprive His children of

---

[69] 1 Cor. 4:3, 4.

their happiness, bidding them sacrifice it and live in sadness. The Apostles felt perfectly safe and confident as they embarked with Christ in their boat, yet they were terrified when the storm arose which seemed likely to drown them, while He, on whose protection they depended, slept and appeared to have forgotten them. But our Lord had not forgotten them; it was His command that raised the tempest, and He was as watchful to deliver them as to place them in danger. Why, then, should you be troubled by the trials your Savior sends you? Why should you dislike the medicine which has come from the hands of your tender Father? Do you think He is austere enough to grieve you, and too weak to deliver you from the afflictions sent by Him? Does He lack mercy, that He will not pardon you and grant you greater graces than ever? Have a strong faith in God's goodness, although to your weak understanding, He seems severe. For your soul, confidence in His mercy is as far superior to distrust as the certainty of faith surpasses the ignorance of human reason.

God gives you these sufferings here to save you from those of eternity. He says of His vineyard: "I keep it night and day, there is no indignation in me against it."[70] He does not permit the sun to injure it by day, nor the moon by night: whether He consoles or afflicts us, He keeps His holy watch over us, and never so faithfully as when we think He has abandoned us.

Trust in God's judgment, dear sister, and not in your own, since He understands what is best for you and knows the present and future state of your soul. Do not weary yourself to death with anxiety, for, as the Gospel says: "You cannot with all your taking thought and caring add one cubit to your stature."[71] Why, then, rely so much on yourself; since God bids you confide in Him? Why struggle so to work out your salvation in your own way, while, after

---

[70] Cf. Isa. 27:3.
[71] Matt. 6:27.

all, God's abundant mercy will avail us far more than our imagined righteousness, when at the last we stand before His judgment.

Close your eyes to all that affrights you and trust in the wounds of Christ, who received them for your sake, and you will find rest. Until the horse ceases looking at the well, for fear of falling in, it will draw no water from it; and so, the more hopeless you feel of a remedy for your troubles, because you know not where to look nor what to do for one, the more hopeful is your state. This is because when human counsel and strength fail, God stretches forth His hand, and that is the hour He was waiting for, in which best to show His mercy. This is to show us that the remedy comes not from our own power, but from the loving and gracious will of God. Therefore, the more our misfortunes accumulate, the more ready and prepared our souls are to receive God's mercy, for the greatness of our misery moves His compassion and causes Him to show the more pity for us.

"He raises up the needy from the earth and lifts up the poor out of the dunghill."[72] He will take from them the sackcloth of affliction and clothe them with the robe of gladness, so that they may confess His loving kindness and mercy. Thus, those who live desolate will praise Him, which greatly pleases Him, as He says: "Call on me in the day of tribulation and I will deliver thee, and thou shalt honor me."[73] Do not be disturbed if that time seems long in coming, for delay is not refusal, especially when the promise has been given by the Truth Himself. Your ears will surely one day hear the words: "Arise, make haste, my love, and come, for winter is now past, the rain is over and gone, the flowers are appearing"[74]—flowers instead of thorns, and your soul shall cast away its mournfulness and bring forth the fruit of love.

---

[72] Cf. Ps. 112:7 (RSV = Ps. 113:7).
[73] Cf. Ps. 49:15 (RSV = Ps. 50:15).
[74] Cant. 2:10-11 (RSV = Song of Sol. 2:10-11).

Finding Confidence in Times of Trial

Remember that on the eve of their deliverance, God's chosen people were afflicted more than they had ever been; burden after burden was laid upon their shoulders, and they were cruelly scourged. So it is that after a night of tempest, the day dawns brightest; after the storm comes the fair weather, and when her travail is over, the mother rejoices in the birth of her child. You must believe that your trials are the heralds of great joy, for no soul deserves to possess peace and the delights of love, until it has been wearied in combat and tasted the bitterness of spiritual desolation.

God is proving you; be faithful to Him, and submit to all He sends you. Love Him, although He chastises you, and follow Him, although He turns away from you. If He answers not, never cease crying to Him, knowing that "you will not labor in vain, for He is faithful and cannot deny Himself and will not despise to the end the prayer of the poor."[75] He will rise and command the sea to be still, and He will give back the living Isaac to you. He will turn your mourning into joy and, after your many fights, will grant you abundance of peace. If your merits do not deserve all this, you will receive it from His bounty.

God asks you to learn to live among the thorns, where there is no place to lay your head; if you can do but little, you must compensate by suffering much. You must walk resolutely in the way of God, for the crown is lost only by those who go astray and renounce it. As for the remedy of your ills, God will give it; *when* and *how* you know not. For the afflictions you bear now you will have a fullness of joy, for which you must bless His Majesty both here and forever in heaven.

---

[75] Cf. 2 Tim. 2:13.

19

To a Student

The Habits for Living a Good Life

I have received your letter, and to tell you the truth, if my many occupations did not often prevent me from answering you, I should ask you to write very frequently, as it is always a great pleasure to receive news of yourself and your family. But as I owe you so much already, let me add this debt to the score, and our Lord will repay you all.

You ask me to tell you how to become a good Christian, and I am most glad to hear your question, for to wish to be a good Christian is to have already started well on the road. But take care not to resemble the many, whose knowledge of God's will, as it does not make them follow it, only condemns them to more severe punishment; for, as Christ tells us: "That servant who knew the will of his lord, and did not according to his will, shall be beaten with many stripes."[76] Therefore, to ask to be shown the way of God is to lay oneself under no small obligation, but as I believe you wish to learn it with the full intention of practicing all that it involves, it is my duty to direct you in it.

Good works are of two kinds. Some are exterior, such as prayer, fasting, and almsgiving; abstaining from swearing, falsehood and

[76] Cf. Luke 12:47.

murmuring; avoiding injuring or annoying people; and other things of a similar kind. Some also are purely spiritual or interior, such as fervent love for God and our neighbor, an intense realization of our own unworthiness, deep gratitude for the divine mercies, and such a profound reverence for the Almighty that we realize our own nothingness in the sight of His greatness. There are also many other religious sentiments which cannot be enumerated. Corporal good works are the easiest to perform, and a man is much to blame if he omits these, for can anyone be careful in greater matters who neglects lesser ones? If we cannot restrain our tongue, or control our bodies and employ them in good works, can we complain that God does not call us to higher things?

The Temple of God in Jerusalem had one gate for the people and further on another through which none but the priests might pass. So, to hear Mass, to honor one's elders, to abstain from speaking or acting wrongly, and other duties of the same kind are common to all Christians, whether they be the friends of God or not; but a heart full of faith and charity is the special gift of His friends and is the distinguishing mark between the sons of perdition and of salvation. As the Jews had to walk through the first portal to reach the second, so Christians pass by good actions to purity of heart. Not that these works in themselves make the heart holy, which can be effected only by the gift of God's grace: but this, by His great mercy, He bestows on those who do their best to serve Him, as far as their weakness will allow them.

What we need, above all other things, is a new heart, but this is the last thing we should think ourselves capable of obtaining by our own power. No man has faith who does not believe that he has received his being from God; neither has he faith who thinks that any other than the Almighty can give him strength to become good, for holiness is a higher gift than mere existence. Those who imagine they can attain to holiness by any wisdom or strength of their own will find themselves, after many labors and struggles and weary efforts, only the farther from possessing it, and this in proportion to their certainty that they of themselves have gained it.

Humility and self-contempt will obtain our wish far sooner than will stubborn pride. Although God is so exalted, His eyes regard the lowly, both in Heaven and on earth, and we shall strive in vain to please Him in any other way than by abasing ourselves. The Son of God came down from heaven and taught us by His life and words the way to Heaven, and that way is humility, as He said: "He that humbleth himself shall be exalted."[77]

Therefore, if you wish God to give you a new heart, you must first of all amend your deeds, and then lament your faults and accuse yourself of your sins. Do not extenuate your defects, but judge yourself justly; let not your self-love blind you, but when conscience accuses you of wrong, do not forget it, but keep it before your eyes and manifest it to Jesus Christ, your Savior and Physician. Weep for it before Him, and He will comfort you without fail. No force can prevail with a Father like the tears of his child, nor is there anything that so moves God to grant us, not justice, but mercy, as our sorrow and self-accusation. Call upon the Almighty, for He will not be deaf to your cries; show Him your wounded soul, for you have not to deal with One who is blind; speak to Him of all your miseries, for He is merciful and will heal them. Go to confession and Holy Communion, and when you are united to your Savior, your soul will melt with devotion, and you will say: "How great is the multitude of thy sweetness O Lord, which thou hast hidden for them that fear thee."[78]

Be sure, too, to show to your neighbor the same love God has shown toward you. If you are harsh to others, you will find God harsh to you, for you know His fixed decree: "With what measure

[77] Luke 18:14.
[78] Ps. 30:20 (RSV = Ps. 31:19).

you mete, it shall be measured to you again."[79] Do not be grudging, then, to other people, lest God treat you in the same way. He will pardon you many crimes for the one offense you forgive your neighbor; He will be long-suffering with you in return for a little patience shown toward others; He will reward you with abundant riches for the small alms you bestow. Strive earnestly, therefore, to keep the law of charity, for in that is your life.

In these few words you see the rule by which you must live: watch carefully over your words and actions. Practice prayer, and beg Christ to grant you a newness and singleness of heart: do nothing to injure others, but rather, do them all the good you can by word and deed, and thus you will fulfill your duty both to God, your neighbor and yourself. "This do and thou shalt live."

Know, however, that if you are to be a friend of God, you must prepare yourself for trials, for without them all your virtue is like an unwalled city, which falls at the first onslaught. Patience is the guardian of all the other virtues, and, if it fail, we may lose in one moment the labor of many days. Our Master and Redeemer tells us: "In your patience you shall possess your souls";[80] without it, we lose control over ourselves, because anger, like wine, robs us of our reason.

Brace up your heart to suffer afflictions, for without the battle there is no victory, and the crown is only for the conqueror. Think not that your burden is heavy; it is very light, compared with what you deserve to have to bear and with what Jesus Christ our Lord bore for your sake; it is slight indeed in comparison with the reward it will bring you. Remember that we shall soon quit this world, and then all the past will seem to us like a short dream, and we shall see that it is better to have labored than to have rested here. Learn how to profit by your sorrows, for they bring great riches to the soul. They cleanse it from past sin; what fire is

[79] Matt. 7:2.
[80] Luke 21:19.

to gold, that tribulation is to the just man, whose heart it purifies. Trials only injure the wicked, for instead of being grateful to God, they murmur against Him. Their punishment does them no good, because they turn their sufferings into sins, and so lose where they might have gained, earning Hell by painful labor. Do not imitate them, but let your courage increase with your trials. God proves His sons by sorrow, and no one will be crowned but he who has been through the combat.

St. James says: "Blessed is the man who endureth temptation, for when he hath been proved, he shall receive the crown of life,"[81] which God promises to those who love Him. If only we realized the value of this crown, how gladly should we now suffer afflictions! Would that we understood how blessed, both now and hereafter, are the tears we shed in this life. We should abase ourselves to the dust here, so that we might stand high in Heaven, and should despise all earthly pleasures, were they given us, in comparison with the heavenly joys for which we hope. Soon the vanity of this world will be unmasked, and the kingdom of God will be revealed. Live here as a stranger—your body on earth, but your heart above—so that when our Lord calls you, He may not find you sleeping, but ready to go with Him, and to hear the sweet words: "Well done, thou good and faithful servant, enter thou into the joy of thy Lord."[82]

[81] Jas. 1:12.
[82] Cf. Matt. 25:21.

20

To a Friend

―――――

On True Charity

You ask me in your letter to tell you in what charity consists, so that you may conform your life to it, for as the apostle says to the Corinthians: "If I should deliver my body to be burned, and have not charity, it profiteth me nothing."[83] You set me no easy task, and it would need St. Paul himself, whose words led you to make the demand, to answer it worthily.

There is nothing of greater importance than charity, and in it consists the perfection of the Christian religion, as the same apostle teaches us: "He that loveth his neighbor hath fulfilled the law."[84] For this reason, pray to the Holy Spirit, whose special attribute is charity, to give you light to understand what it is, as He did to the Apostles on the day of Pentecost when He infused it into their hearts, since He and no other can teach it to us. For how can a mortal man speak the language of Heaven, which is understood only by the blessed, whose whole affections are occupied in loving God and whatever else He desires them to love? How can I, who come of Adam's race and inherit a tendency to seek myself in all things, speak to you of that love which is fixed on God alone, and

―――――

[83] 1 Cor. 13:3.
[84] Rom. 13:8.

entirely forgets its own interests? We even perform many religious duties with a view to our own profit, so that often, however holy the work may be, it is prompted by self-love alone. For as water flows to the same place, whether it passes through a golden or an earthenware conduit, so, whether our actions be good or bad, our motive tends through them toward our own interests.

May Jesus Christ, who always sought God's honor, and whose love made Him come down to earth, to do not His own will, but the will of His Father who sent Him, loose my tongue, for I should not dare to speak on such a subject but at your desire, which urges me to endeavor to tell you something of what I have read.

The best way to possess true charity and understand what it is, is to consider how the blessed in heaven practice it, because the more closely we imitate them, the more perfect shall we be in that virtue. The love that the saints bear toward God transforms their will, so that it becomes one with His: that is, they can wish, or not wish, only what He does; because, as St. Denis says, one effect of love is to make the will of those who love one, and God's whole love and will are centered upon His own glory and essence, which is supremely perfect. It therefore follows that the love of the saints is that single-minded affection and will with which they long, with all their strength, that God may be in Himself as good and glorious and adorable as He is. Seeing Him to possess all these perfections, they feel an ineffable joy, which is the fruit of the Holy Spirit.

It will give us some idea of what this happiness is if we consider how a good son rejoices in seeing his father rich, powerful, wise, beloved, and respected by all, and honored by the king. Indeed, some children are so dutiful that no troubles or misfortunes of their own can destroy the pleasure they feel in their parents' prosperity, which they consider of the first importance.

Now, if this human joy for a parent be so great, what must be the jubilation of the saints, transformed as they are by heavenly

love, at beholding that God is so holy, perfect, and rich in
lence. They see that, as Creator of the universe, He, by one .
act of His will, gave all things their beauty and being and upl. ..is
them in existence, so that not a single leaf can rustle in the wind
but by His consent. Behold the joy "such as eye hath not seen, nor
ear heard, neither hath it entered into the heart of man."[85]

This, then, as far as it is possible for us to understand it, is the
"charity" of the just in heaven. From this overflowing river that
gladdens the city of God comes, as a streamlet, their love for their
neighbor. Their one longing and joy is to see the God they love
so fervently possess all glory and honor, and hence, they ardently
desire that the blessed, their companions, may be as full of beauty
and felicity, as they are themselves, because God is thus honored
in them. For this reason, they delight more in the perfections of
the greatest saints than in their own, because they see that they
give God the higher praise, thus showing how far they are above
the envy that springs from self-love.

But, perhaps you will say, they may feel some sorrow at finding themselves in a lower degree of sanctity than others, since
it prevents them from giving so much honor to their Creator as
they might have done. You must remember, however, that the
first effect of their love of God is to unite their wills with His, so as
to accord fully with His desires; thus, they are content with what
they possess, seeing that it is His will that one soul should exceed
another in glory. The city of God is embellished by having diver-
sity of rank among the saints, as a violin produces sweeter music
for having many strings of different notes than it could do, had
it but one. As the blessed perceive that, by there being different
mansions and degrees of glory in the triumphant Church, it gains
in beauty and that thereby their Lord's honor is increased, they
are not troubled by being in a lower state themselves than others

[85] 1 Cor. 2:9.

of their company; for they, with their paler tints, and the others with their richer colors, blend together in their united manifestation of the infinite love and beauty of their Creator. This is the river that St. John saw in the Apocalypse, issuing from the throne of God and of the Lamb;[86] from this the blessed drink, and, inebriated with love, sing their everlasting *Alleluia*, praising and blessing our Lord God. This is, as it were, the enamel that decorates those precious stones of which is built the Temple of the heavenly Jerusalem.

Now, my dear sister, such is the sanctuary you must make in your heart as a dwelling-place for God, as Moses was commanded to see and make the Tabernacle according to the pattern that was shown to him on the mount.[87] If you intend to pass through this life in perfect charity and love of God, you must, as far as possible, constantly desire that He may be in Himself good, as holy and as full of excellence as indeed He is. It must be a continual joy and feast to your soul to consider God's attributes and think how He contains in Himself all power and perfection, and how, although all creatures possess their being from Him and cannot exist without Him, yet He has no need of them. This must be the end you should strive to attain, and in this, as St. Thomas says, consists perfect charity. The feeling of tender devotion toward God which beginners call charity, although holy, is not of so high a degree of purity as that which unites souls with their Beloved.

Holy Scripture frequently invites us to this love, as in the ninety-sixth psalm we find, "Rejoice ye just, in the Lord."[88] St. Paul too writes: "Rejoice in the Lord," and not content with enjoining it once, he repeats the counsel saying, "Again I say rejoice."[89] David also cries: "Delight in the Lord, and He will give thee the

---

[86] Apoc. 22:1 ff. (RSV = Rev. 22:1 ff.).
[87] Exod. 25:40.
[88] Ps. 96:12 (RSV = Ps. 97:12).
[89] Phil. 4:4.

requests of thy heart."[90] This is the joy the most holy Virgin felt when she sang: "My spirit hath rejoiced in God my Savior"[91] and which our Lord Himself experienced, when, as St. Luke writes, Jesus "rejoiced in the Holy Spirit."[92] The royal prophet also tells us: "My heart and my flesh have rejoiced in the living God."[93] The "heart" here signifies the will, and this happens when it is actually engaged in loving and desiring that God may possess those good things which are indeed His. Sometimes this joy so overflows the soul that the body itself is inflamed with devotion toward its Creator. It is so excellent and divine that the Church, which is guided by the Holy Spirit, invites us to practice it in the Invitatory of Matins, exclaiming: "Come let us praise the Lord with joy: let us joyfully sing to God our Savior."[94]

If you would prove its excellence, practice it, and you will find the soul cannot satisfy itself without praising God. Seeing that God possesses all that the soul desires Him to have, it immediately breaks forth into thanksgiving to Him. This is the same effect that follows with the blessed in Heaven, according to the Psalm: "Blessed are they that dwell in thy house, O Lord, they shall praise thee forever and ever."[95] So ardently did St. Augustine's heart burn with this love, that he exclaimed: "If Thou, O Lord, wert Augustine, and I God, I would make Thee God, and myself Augustine." There is no need for further instances to prove the excellence of this love, which is manifestly that which draws a man out of himself and unites him to the Deity.

Therefore, my dear sister, let your actions and devotions be directed to the glory and honor of God, who deserves that all

---

[90] Ps. 36:4 (RSV = Ps. 37:4).
[91] Luke 1:47.
[92] Luke 10:21.
[93] Ps. 83:3 (RSV = Ps. 84:2).
[94] Ps. 94:1 (RSV = Ps. 95:1).
[95] Ps. 83:5 (RSV = Ps. 84:4).

His creatures should serve and adore Him for His own good-ness alone, without looking for any recompense for themselves. Although it is right and holy to perform our good works with the hope of future reward, perfect charity rather seeks the honor and glory of our Lord God, and this should be our chief intention. We may sometimes, however, consider the blessings to be reaped for ourselves, so as to animate our fervor in good works; thus, you may say with David: "I have inclined my heart, for the reward, to do thy justifications for ever."[96]

But perhaps you will ask "How can the soul, which is often sad and tepid, have strength constantly to rejoice and exult in the Lord? How can it always feel such perfect and sovereign love?" As I have already told you, charity consists in the unwavering desire that God should possess in Himself all the perfections proper to Him, and this the heart can wish for, even though it may be dry and sorrowful; just as a son can hope for his father's happiness, however unfortunate he is himself. I allow that for this there is need of the grace of God, but He never refuses that grace to those who endeavor to walk in this way. If He wishes to communicate more intimately with the soul, He also gives it a joy and exulta-tion that is the fruit of the Holy Spirit.

When His Majesty bestows this favor upon us, let us thank Him for it; but when He does not vouchsafe to do so, let us perse-vere in striving to bless, worship, and adore Him as He deserves. It is in that act of the will that charity consists, and it is a great error to think that unless it is accompanied by feelings of joy, it is worthless. The Devil knows this and is always trying to make us feel lukewarm and dry, so that we may give up this holy practice. Persevere in it, and stop your ears to his temptations, or you will never gain the crown in Heaven that those who are advanced in this holy love wear even on earth. Keep constant watch that

---

[96] Cf. Ps. 118:112 (RSV = Ps. 119:112).

you do indeed make God's honor your real end, for so great is the bias toward self-love inherited with fallen nature, that sometimes you will find yourself seeking self, even when acting with this intention—by rejoicing at your affection for Him, because of its reward in Heaven, or because of the consolation it brings to your soul, or for other selfish motives, which would mar the perfection of your charity.

Now that you see how your love for God is to be modeled on that of the saints in Heaven, I will explain the love of your neighbor that should spring from it. It consists in loving his virtues and desiring them for him, so that God may be glorified in him. Your pleasure should augment in proportion as his sanctity increases, and you should regret his sins as offenses against his Creator. For since the love of God consists in wishing Him well, and rejoicing in His perfections, so fraternal charity is an act of the will by which we wish well to others, rejoice in their true good, and feel sorry for their faults. This is a great grace our Lord bestows upon whom He chooses. The love for God and man, then, both concur to the one end that God may be praised and worshiped.

This shows how far he fails in charity who grieves to see others make more progress in perfection than himself. Although our hearts should be deeply wounded at seeing that we do not serve God as we ought and might, yet they should be consoled by seeing others render Him the homage in which we are wanting. To feel regret at this can spring only from self-love, for, if we desire only God's glory, we can but rejoice at seeing others give it to Him.

Now, dear sister, you see what you must do in the paradise of the Church Militant, in which God placed you when He called you to His love and grace, if you would hope to receive the reward that will be given to the Church Triumphant in glory, in which I beseech our Lord that we may all worship and praise and enjoy Him for all eternity. Amen.

21

To a Young Lady

On Preparation for Christmas —
How to Receive the Christ Child

How busily employed you must be during this holy season in preparing a lodging for the Guest who is coming to you! I fancy I can see you, as solicitous as Martha, and yet as peaceful as Magdalene, preparing to give to your coming Savior the service both of soul and body; and He is worthy of both, for He is your God. O blessed time, which brings before our minds the truth that God came in the flesh to dwell among us, to enlighten our darkness, and to direct our feet in the way of peace, so that, being made His brethren, we might share in His inheritance!

Earnestly indeed may you long for Christ's advent, and prepare your heart to be His dwelling-place, for men wished for His coming ages before His birth, so that the prophet styles Him "the Desired of all nations."[97] Jesus gives Himself to none but those who eagerly look for Him. Choice food is thrown away on such as cannot taste it, and so those who long not after God's presence cannot value Him as they ought.

Our Lord hears "the desire of the poor"[98] and bends His ear to listen to the sighing of their hearts after Him, for that is all He

[97] Agg. 2:8 (RSV = Hag. 2:8).
[98] Ps. 9:17 (RSV = Ps. 10:17).

cares for in the children of men. When their sighs reach Him, He comes into their souls; nor can He refuse Himself, for, as He tells us in the Canticle, "Thou hast wounded my heart, my sister, my spouse, thou hast wounded my heart with one of thy eyes and with one hair of thy neck."[99] What can be more tender than that which is wounded by a glance of the eye, or weaker than what is bound by a single hair? How can men say that God is difficult to find, or rigorous in His treatment of us, or hard to bear with? Bitterly should we blame ourselves for caring to look on anything but on Him, and for not closing our eyes upon creatures so as in spirit to contemplate God.

The archer shuts one eye when shooting, the better to hit the target, but we will not turn our sight from creatures to be able to follow and wound our Lord with love. The soul that wishes to find God must withdraw its affections from all else and place them entirely in Him, for God is love, and it is only by love that He can be ensnared. He will have nothing to do with those who have it not, and if they say they know Him as they ought, St. John will tell them that they speak not the truth.[100] But our Lord, who is wounded by a glance, is bound by a single hair, for that which is conquered by love is kept by recollection and contemplation.

In order that men might feel confident that they can find God, and certainty that He will not desert them afterward, He made Himself one of them and laid Himself in the arms of a Virgin, bound hand and foot in swaddling bands, so that He could not flee from those who came in quest of Him.

O celestial Bread, descended from the bosom of the Father, who remains on Your altars throughout the world, inviting all to come and feast on You, and enjoy You! Who could refrain from seeking You and receiving You into his bosom — You who asks

---

[99] Cant. 4:9 (RSV = Song of Sol. 4:9).
[100] 1 John 4:8.

only that man should hunger for You, to bestow Yourself on him? What do You require of the soul, but only that it should sigh after You and, confessing its sins, should beg You to come and dwell within it?

How miserable are those who, when this Bread descends close to their very doors, prefer rather to die of hunger than to stoop to pick it up. O sloth, what evil you work! What riches does not such blindness lose for souls! What treasures does not their slumber steal away from them! God has promised that "every one that asketh, receiveth; and he that seeketh findeth, and to him that knocketh, it shall be opened."[101] What but our own negligence is to blame if we lose His mercies? Shall we cling to our infirmities, now that God comes to cure them? He stands at the door of our hearts, begging and imploring of us: "Open to me, my sister, my love!"[102] And we, so engrossed by our vanities that we will not rise to let Him in, leave Him there with the cry upon His lips.

Come here, my soul, and tell me, in the name of God, what is it that hinders you from giving yourself entirely to Him? For what do you care if it be not for this Spouse of yours? Why do you not love dearly Him who has such a mighty love for you? It was solely out of affection for you that He came to dwell on earth, and to gain your profit by His own loss. Why are you placed in this world, save to live in mutual love with the King of Heaven? Do you not understand how everything on earth will pass away? What is all that you see, or hear, or touch, or taste; what are all those among whom you live? They are in truth but as cobwebs, which cannot clothe thee, nor shield thee from the cold. Where are you when you are not with Jesus Christ? What do you think of, or value, or seek for, outside of Him alone, who is the only perfect good?

---

[101] Matt. 7:8.
[102] Cant. 5:2 (RSV = Song of Sol. 5:2).

Finding Confidence in Times of Trial

Let us arise and shake off this evil dream; let us awake, for it is day, and Christ, who is the light, is come; let us, who were wont to do the works of darkness, do the works of day. Oh! that we might so bitterly repent of the time we spent in ignorance of God, that the memory of it might spur us on to speed the more swiftly after Him. Would that we might run, and fly to Him, and that we might burn with an ardor such as to transform us into Him. What should not we poor creatures do, when we see our Creator become man solely because of His love for us! What passion was ever so strong as to convert the lover into the likeness of his beloved? God showed that we were dear to Him when He made us after His own image, but far stronger was the proof He gave of His love, when He made Himself in the image of man. He abased Himself to raise us to His level; He became man to make us as gods; He descended from heaven that He might raise us to dwell there with Him, and above all, He died to give us life. And shall we lie slumbering, and make Him no return for this great love?

Enlighten my eyes, O Lord, that they may not sleep in death, and You, who hast granted us these mercies, make us duly grateful for them, lest the very greatness of Your gifts should turn to our deeper condemnation. Open my eyes, O Lord, that I may see You descending from the bosom of the Father into that of Your Virgin Mother, so that I may thank You as I ought and humble myself before You. Let me look on You, lying with a manger for Your cradle, sobbing with the cold and oppressed by poverty, that I may be willing to surrender all luxuries for Your sake. Let Your cries resound in my ears and soften my heart, so that it may be as wax in Your hands. Do not permit God to weep, and man to be indifferent to His tears, for I know not which of these two things is to be more dreaded.

Seal up, O Christ, Your words in my soul, so that it may not sin against You. Gather up the blood You shed for me, and pour it into my heart; let my love be wholly Yours as a return for all

Your sufferings for me. It was for me that You sought; for me that You fought; for me that You bore the mockings and all that cost You so dear. Let me be all Yours, since You have ransomed me so dearly. God, who is about to be born, has no house or cradle ready for Him, so do you prepare your heart for His dwelling-place. Let it be warm with love, for the Babe is chilled; but still, if it be only tepid, the shivering Infant will bring it greater heat. The more He suffers from the cold for us, the more strongly does He prove His love and so deserves our love still more. In the rigorous winter weather, which He bore for us, He chose to wear no clothes to protect Him; but naked was He born, and naked died upon the Cross for us, because, in both His birth and death, He manifested the greatest excess of love. You must have ready a crib, then, in which to rock him to sleep, which symbolizes the repose of contemplation. See that you treat Him well, for He is the Son of a mighty King and of a Virgin, and loves to dwell in the breasts of virgins, for the food that pleases Him is mortified and crucified nature.

He has many poor brethren, and those who love Him must love them too, for His sake. Give them your alms, for they are the brothers of your Creator.

When our Lord comes to be born in your soul, keep careful guard over Him, and may He protect and save you for His mercy's sake. Amen.

22

To a Friend

*On Preparation for Epiphany —
the Gold of Divine Love*

I wrote to you in Advent about the great mercy our Lord showed in deigning to visit us, and the happiness of the soul to whom He comes. I hope that in His mercy He has come to you and that you have received Him with faith and love. Offer yourself, then, wholly, as a perpetual sacrifice to Him who has deigned to be your loving guest; and since you have toiled like the magi in seeking the Divine Child, imitate them in their faith and in their gifts to Him when they found Him. Contemplate God Himself, humbly lying in a crib within a stable, where human reason would never have led the Kings to look for Him.

The star, which is faith, stopped above the cave and declared by its resplendent rays, as by so many tongues, that here, concealed from man's understanding, He lay hidden, who is above all our science and understanding. So does the star, which is faith, teach us to believe the more firmly where there appear least grounds to do so. For if these travelers had been led by their reason instead of by the star, they would have sought the newborn King in a royal palace as the most suitable abode for Him. Our Lord gives a great grace to those to whom He manifests the star of the light of faith, so that, like the magi, they may find Him hidden in the swaddling clothes and amid the poverty of His Birth, or, as did the good thief, in the ignominy and death of the cross. If the three Kings had believed our Lord to be but an earthly sovereign, however great, they would merely have paid Him the respect due from one man to another, but faith revealed to them the Incarnate God concealed beneath the appearance of a newborn Babe, and they adored Him, prostrate on the ground, confessing their own nothingness in His presence.

Take care not to appear empty-handed before our Lord, and think not that you are giving Him anything, if you give not your love. Nothing but God can make you happy, nor can anything you offer Him but yourself satisfy Him. His is not a mercenary love that regards the value of the gift, but it is that true and perfect love, which is the union of hearts. This, as St. Bernard says, is when God and the soul speak in accord. For if the Almighty should threaten or punish me, I must not do the like to Him, but, when He manifests His power, humble myself the more. But if He give me His love, I am bound to return it, crying with the Spouse: "My beloved to me, and I to him."[103]

What an honor for the creature to be united to its Creator in such a bond of mutual love; this indeed is what Isaiah tells us "levels mountains and raises valleys."[104] Offer your heart to Christ, whose tender mercy for us led Him, although the infinite God, to become a man — nay, an infant — and who, not satisfied with shedding tears when He was born, eight days after shed His blood for us.[105]

Since you so entirely belong to our Lord, do not rob Him of yourself, lest you be found among those of whom the prophet Jeremiah says: "They walked in their own will and in the perversity

[103] Cant. 2:16 (RSV = Song of Sol. 2:16).
[104] Cf. Isa. 40:4.
[105] Luke 2:21.

of their own wicked heart."[106] To whom else should you give yourself? Where else would you be better off? How can you exalt yourself more highly than by loving Jesus, who loved you and washed you in His blood, and who gives Himself to those who desire Him, making them from men to become as gods?

Be careful, then, to offer gold to the Infant Jesus. For as a little gold is worth more than a great quantity of the baser metals, so a little gold of true love is far more precious than all the copper of fear and self-interest, with the actions springing from them. Many people value themselves in proportion to the number of their good works, forgetting that God cares more for the motive of our actions than for their quantity, and that far fewer works would be better pleasing to Him, were they accompanied by warmer love. With love, a small alms or a fast from one meal only will content Him better than much greater austerities and gifts without it. So the widow who gave her two mites pleased Him better than many who gave far more, because of her truer love. God's greatness appears in this: that no service, however great counts for much before Him if not rendered with the whole heart. For why should He, who has need of nothing, and who cannot increase in riches or in any other good, care for anything that can be given to Him, except for the love of the giver, which is so precious a present that none can rightly refuse it?

This gift God desires so strongly that He punishes with eternal death all who withhold it from Him. Who can be so little covetous as He who has no need of anything we can offer Him? Or who is there that longs for our hearts as keenly as God does, seeing that He sends to Hell those who refuse them to Him? Even if we love Him, He is not contented unless we prefer Him above all else. St. Augustine cried: "Lord, Thou commandest me to love Thee, and dost threaten me with misery unless I do so!"

---

[106] Jer. 7:24.

Let your chief care be to love our Lord. It is for this that He made Himself so little, for the more He dissembles His Majesty, the more He shows us His goodness and thus invites our love, which we are more drawn to give Him in the littleness that He took upon Him than in the majesty that is His own. His wisdom was hidden when He became an infant without power of speech; His power appeared as if bound by the swaddling clothes, as He lay upon the hay, suffering from the bitter cold. All this He did, because the more He hid His other attributes, the more He manifested His tenderness for us, so that we might love Him the better for what He endured for us. For, surely, when we see Him tremble with cold, it draws our hearts to Him more than if we saw Him warmly clad and free from suffering.

Therefore, if we refuse our hearts to the divine Babe whose devotion to us cost Him so dear, we shall have a heavy fine to pay. He who gives his affections to God offers what David terms "the holocaust with its marrow";[107] for as fire consumes the whole sacrificial victim, so does love consume the whole man, both within and without, and its flames do not leave unburned the straws of exterior vanities. How can he whose heart is given to the Infant Jesus bring himself to care for pomp and show, for those who love grow to resemble one another? Since God bestowed on us such a favor in coming down to show Himself to us as our way, let us travel to heaven in the footsteps of Him who is the Truth, and not run in the treacherous path of the world, which would lead us to Hell.

Let our holocaust contain marrow, which is soft and quickly melted, like the heart given to God, which should have nothing hard or sharp in it toward either Him or its neighbors. And as the marrow is protected from injury, first by the skin, then by the flesh, and lastly is encased within the hard bone itself; so should

[107] Cf. Ps. 65:15 (RSV = Ps. 66:15).

charity be guarded by the devout soul at the risk of losing all it possesses; and the will, hard as the bone, should resolutely defend, at any cost, its love for our Lord.

Such must be the gold you offer to the Infant, who chose to be born so poor. Open then, your caskets, as did the magi; for if your heart, which is your treasure-house, be kept shut, all your labor is lost. All else is not gold but tinsel, and you would keep the best for yourself and give our Lord the worst. Open your heart, then, and place in it the newborn Infant, for without Him it cannot be said to live. He is not a burden; hold Him, then, fast to your breast as the Spouse did her "bundle of myrrh."[108] Treat Him with all reverence, for He is your God; yet you may dare to speak to Him, for He is a child and is as sweet and gentle as He looks. Beware lest you let Him go, for it requires great care to keep Him. You must love Him dearly, or you will either forget Him, or He will weary you. Do not rest until you feel sure of your love for one another. Until the soul knows this, it lives in fear and sadness beneath the weight of the Law, but when once the soul realizes that God dwells in it, and the soul in Him, there is little that can trouble it. May this be accomplished in you. Amen.

---

[108] Cant. 1:12 (RSV = Song of Sol. 1:12).

23

To a Devout Friend

On Preparation for Lent—A Meditation on
Humility, Pride, and the Perfect Love of God

May God bless you during this Lent and grant that you may receive the ashes upon your forehead at the beginning of this holy season with such fitting dispositions as to preserve constantly that holy humility in your heart which they betoken. He to whom God gives light to understand and to sorrow for the state he was in while he lived apart from his Creator is delivered from the total blindness of pride and is made capable of receiving all fitting spiritual graces. The Holy Scriptures say: "Pride is the beginning of all sin; he that holdeth it shall be filled with maledictions";[109] that is to say, "vices." For as a king is rarely seen alone, so, many other sins usually accompany pride, and neither does humility keep solitary state; for, as St. James tells us: "God giveth grace to the humble,"[110] and grace is the mother of all the virtues.

Pride seeks after honors and is grieved when it is despised; humility is averse to being treated well and rejoices in contempt, which it knows that it deserves, and its own uprightness renders it desirous that justice should be done. Pride never has what it

---

[109] Ecclus. 10:15 (RSV = Sir. 10:12-13).
[110] James 4:6.

wants, for whatever it possesses, or has given to it, it considers that it deserves still more; while humility always thinks it has more than enough, for it believes that it is unworthy to walk the earth, and that hell itself is not sufficient punishment for its sins. Pride can live in peace with no one, not even with itself, while humility agrees with all men, for it abases itself before everyone and bears patiently with them, believing with all its heart that they are better than itself. Pride finds it insupportable to submit to others, whether to God or to a mortal creature, but humility gives way and bows down, so that it is able to pass through the "narrow gate" of obeying the will of God and man.

Great are the blessings that come to us with the ashes of humility; let no man be without it, lest he be without God also, for, as St. Augustine exclaims: "Behold how high Thou art, O Lord, and yet dost dwell with the lowly of heart!" The prophet also says: "To whom shall I have respect but to him that is poor and little, and that trembleth at my words?"[111] Humility, which makes a man think basely of himself, is yet no base thing, nor is it a fruit that springs from this earth, but grows in Heaven. God bestows it on those who search deeply in the mire of their own souls, and diligently turn over in their minds the remembrance of their sins and frailties, for it is among such needs and miseries that this precious jewel is usually discovered. Our frequent errors have given us so many transgressions to examine into and to repent of, that, unless he willfully turn away his eyes from himself, there is no man who will not see ample reasons not only to be humbled, but to be confounded, at his own imperfections. Woe be to us if we be one of those of whom God says: "Thou hadst a harlot's forehead, thou wouldst not blush"; or again, speaking of others: "They were not confounded with confusion."[112] For what can be more revolting than to meet with insolence in one who should be

[111] Isa. 66:2.
[112] Jer. 3:3; 6:15.

filled with shame? Who dare lift his eyes to God or to His creatures, if he consider how he has offended against them both? Is
there one among us who has not failed in the perfect love of God,
for we do not love Him with all our understanding and with all
our mind by believing His word implicitly and by devoting all our
wishes, thoughts, and purposes to serving Him more fervently. He
who loves Him with his whole heart gives no part of it either to
himself or to other men, loving none save for God, and in God,
and so renouncing all self-interest as to love God purely for His
own sake.

Let each one think how little he has mortified his passions,
and how he resists the reign of God's love within him, and he will
see that he does not love God with all his soul. Our Lord commands us to love Him with all our strength, and indeed we ought
to beg His pardon for our weakness in this respect; our energies
are given to our own interests, and the concupiscence that dwells
within us makes us fail to serve God diligently, and love Him
fervently.

St. Augustine says that, as charity grows, concupiscence dimin-
ishes, and that no evil desires can exist with perfect charity. By
the word *desires*, he means the immoderate self-love we all bear
toward ourselves. Now, as, with the exception of Jesus Christ our
Lord, and His most holy Mother, no member of the race of Adam
has ever been altogether without some degree of this inordinate
self-love, none but they have ever been perfect in divine love. If
selfishness has killed the love of God, then we are in a state of
mortal sin; while if the love of God lives and reigns in our souls,
making them resolute not to offend Him mortally, they are in a
state of grace. If, however, self and creatures usurp an undue place
in our affections, our charity is not perfect. Our works are imperfect if this virtue is defective, since it is that which gives them life.

When we do not love God as we should, we are wanting also
in the love of our neighbors, for we neither feel compassion for

the sorrow nor joy at the happiness of those who are very near and dear to God, and who were made His adopted children in Baptism. We do not behave toward them with due charity, because we are imperfect in our love for Him who said: "As long as you did it to one of these my least brethren, you did it to me."[113]

Although many of our actions may be not only free from sin, but good in themselves, and, being done in a state of grace, may merit eternal life, yet for want of this twofold charity, which is the root of all good, these works may have many defects. If you would be truthful and humble, you must give God glory for all the good you do and thank Him for having aided your free will to choose rightly, and for giving you the power to merit by using the grace He has mercifully bestowed on you. Nevertheless, you must examine the faults you have committed in these actions, for it is safer to think of our failings than of our virtues. Be sure that, however strict your search may be, enough evil will still escape your notice to give you cause to cry with contrition to God: "From my secret sins cleanse me, O Lord."[114] This is the reason we do not love our neighbors in the way God wishes, nor as much as He desires, and that we do not bear patiently with them and try to avoid annoying them. In fact, this is the origin of all the shortcomings that pollute our soul like a festering wound. Our sins are greater than the human intellect can realize, and only our Creator, who sees to the bottom of our heart, knows all its weakness; for often that which seems perfect to us is very evil in His sight.

Therefore, as Job says, we should "fear all our works,"[115] and however right they may seem to us, we must not be contented with them, nor allow ourselves a secret complacency in them. The self-contented conscience does not content God; and that man alone is just before Him, who knows that all justice and

[113] Matt. 25:40.
[114] Ps. 18:13 (RSV = Ps. 19:12).
[115] Cf. Job 9:28.

grace proceed from the divine mercy. Nothing so offends its Creator as a self-satisfied heart, because it contains no empty vessel into which He can pour the riches of His mercy. It will remain in its natural poverty, for it can offer no place into which the waters of grace may flow, to make it live happily with God, and bring forth much fruit, like a well-watered garden.

All things that we possess proceed from God, and if anyone thinks he can so much as say "the Lord Jesus!" of his own power, he puts himself in God's place, for he attributes to himself what his Creator alone can do. God gives Himself to us on the condition that we confess the truth, that in Him and from Him, and not from ourselves, comes all that we have. The greater the good we possess, the deeper is our debt toward the Almighty, and the stronger reason have we to blame ourselves for not corresponding to such signal mercies by more generous service, and to greater graces with a warmer gratitude. He who is taught by divine truth attributes nought to himself save his sins and his own nothingness. If all that God gave us at our creation, and which by His power He daily sustains, were withdrawn from us, there would remain only nothingness and we should return to the nothingness from which we were formed. And if God took from us the grace which He bestows on us for the sake of Jesus Christ, what would the most holy among us be, but what Peter was when he denied our Lord, or Paul when he persecuted his Redeemer? We know but too well what we were before God touched our souls, and taking from us our old hearts gave us new ones in their stead.

Justification is nothing but the resurrection of a soul that was dead in sin, and henceforth exists by the life that God infuses into it through the death of His blessed Son. It would be madness if the body attributed its animation and power of motion to itself and not to the spirit which dwells in it and quickens it; and the soul is as blind which thinks that its good works come from its own abilities, and not from the supernatural life divinely bestowed on it. Sometimes such presumption draws down chastisement from Heaven, and the gifts possessed by the soul are withdrawn, so that it finds itself unable to see, to hear, to take pleasure in religious matters, or to perform the good actions it was wont to do. Thus, the Christian soul discovers that it was another Being who gave it the spiritual life it did but receive, and that without the grace of Jesus Christ it is like a corpse from which animation has fled.

You see, then, my friend, that your defects are all that you can attribute to yourself, for you possess nothing else of your own. If our Lord afflict you, think how weak and faulty you must be, to show so little resignation at His just punishment. If He send you consolations, be confused at the want of humility you manifest in the way you accept them, for the more God honors you and treats you as if you were righteous, the more should you abase yourself, and be ashamed of your shortcomings. Remember how little you profit by the inspirations and promptings you receive from God, and how often, when He urges you again and again to do something for Him, you forget His wish almost at once and do not carry it out. Surely His every word should remain imprinted in your memory for life, without need for Him to repeat it. Think how often your faulty heart lets the precious grace that our Lord pours into it become wasted, instead of carefully preserving it.

When God gives us spiritual sweetness, we should prepare our souls to receive it again by withdrawing more from earthly joys, and by keeping our minds closed against them and more recollected and given to God; yet it sometimes happens that these very graces only cause our souls to be more given to external things than ever, because of the levity of our natures. An examination of our failings must make us confess that we do nothing well, and that we have more cause to blush for the many defects in all our actions, than to think for a moment that we have done anything praiseworthy.

If a page does not show due respect to the king he waits on, if he answers not immediately when he is spoken to, or if he be slow in delivering any message, he will certainly be punished. So too, those we serve are not content at our merely doing their bidding, but, unless we do it well, we shall be blamed and disgraced.

Which of us can say that he treats God with the reverence He deserves? Or whose soul trembles within him while he adores that ineffable Majesty as, we are told in the holy Mass, "the Powers tremble"? Where is the shame we should feel before that infinite Wisdom, who knows what we are and sees all that is within us? Where can obedience be found such as needs no second bidding? Where a prudence that shows the soul how best to serve and please the Almighty? Have Christians a fitting gratitude for His numberless and unspeakable benefits, or do they give such a mighty God and Master that service of soul and body which is His due? If anyone truthfully judge himself, he will see how deeply sunk he is in sin and misery. At night, when the time comes to examine his conscience as to the actions of the past day, he will find that all his words and works, his thoughts and deeds, are full of faults, and that he has left undone much good that he might have done, because he has not rightly loved God or his neighbor; he will recognize his ingratitude toward God, and his impatience in bearing with others; and he will discover that he has omitted to practice innumerable other virtues. If, by the divine help, he has performed any good works, they are either stained with pride, vainglory, or tepidity, or he has not fully corresponded to divine grace.

In short, God's light will show him a thousand blemishes in his conduct, and he will feel sure that there are as many more he has failed to discover; understanding the weakness of his nature, he will suspect that he knows not half the worst. The humble Christian thinks his own wickedness as inconceivable as is God's goodness. Should any divine favors be shown him, far from attributing them to any merit of his own, he blames himself for not corresponding to them and profiting by them as he ought. Thus, he sincerely gives God his due, which is all that he possesses which is good and unsullied by any admixture of evil. Convinced of this truth, as revealed by God Himself, the lowly spirit, rising above itself, ceases to depend upon such a broken reed as itself and leans for support on Him who upholds all things. Looking within his soul, the Christian sees cause only for repentance, and so lifts his eyes to his Creator, in whose loving kindness he can trust without fear of being forsaken. God is so faithful that He never abandons those who have recourse to Him; His love is so tender that far sooner will the sea run dry, or the sun cease shining, than the heavenly Father lack pity for His own. Therefore do they run and fly because God carries them; they stumble not, for He upholds them; they err not, for He is their guide, and never will they be condemned, for He gives His kingdom to those who "become as little children."[116]

Take heed to yourself, then, since our Lord so urgently demands it of you; give glory to God for what is praiseworthy, but impute to yourself all that deserves blame and dishonor. Place all your hopes of perseverance in the right way in our Lord, who did not set you in it with the intention of deserting you halfway, but seeks to lead you by it into the company of His spouses in Paradise. There He will heap honors upon you, so do not seek for honors here. With a celestial feast in prospect, you should not satiate yourself with the filth of this world: nothing can please the palate that has once tasted of that heavenly banquet. Turn away from all that you will so soon be forced to leave, and set not your heart on anything so transitory. You would be bearing little enough for God, if you alone had to endure all possible sufferings. Think of the Hell your sins have deserved, and of the Paradise our

[116] Matt. 18:3.

Lord means you to enjoy, since He has put you on the road that leads to it. Contemplate the pains Christ bore for your sake, and you will deem all that you do or may suffer for Him unworthy of a second thought. God should be so precious to you that nothing He costs you should seem worth considering; even if you purchased Him with your life, so small a price should count as nothing. In Heaven you will realize what an advantageous exchange you made and how foolish those poor wretches were who set their hearts on the transitory good, and gave themselves up to pleasure, oblivious of God's promises. What fervent thanks you will render to Divine Providence, for having enlightened you when you were deceived as they are, and drawn your thoughts above this earth. You were the slave of vanity when our heavenly Father adopted you for His son: you were living without thought of God's promised mercies when He placed you where you now are and so gave you the right to trust that He will be your succor both in life and in death.

Then, after this exile is ended, He will set you in the land of the living, in the clear fruition of the Beatific Vision. What your joy will be God alone can tell, as He alone is able and willing to bestow it. This will He do, not for your own merits but because "He is good, for His mercy endureth for ever,"[117] and to him be glory and praise for all, and from all, and in all, forever and ever. Amen.

---

[117] Ps. 105:1 (RSV = Ps. 106:1).

24

To a Friend

On Pentecost — Preparing a Place for the Holy Spirit

God grant you to realize the happiness of Whitsuntide, not only by hearsay, but by experiencing in your heart what was felt by Christ's faithful servants assembled in the Cenacle, when the Holy Spirit was poured into their souls. He so strengthened their weakness, enlightened their ignorance, and filled them with joy, that all could see that our Lord's blood had not been shed in vain, but had gained them, through His prayers, a participation in the divine nature.

When they felt themselves thus transformed by grace and saw how wonderfully God loved them, they had such an ardent love for Him that they sang forth praises to Christ their Lord and Master, for having, as God, sent them this gift, which, as man, He had earned for them. They remembered His promise that the Holy Spirit would come to make Him known and bear testimony of Him to the disciples and the world, to teach all that every good comes through Him alone, so that all might feel bound to render Him service and gratitude, as their most true and generous Benefactor. Because of this they loved Him even better after His departure, than while He was among them, and felt so great an affection infused by the Holy Spirit into their souls for the Word of God, from whom He proceeds and in whom He reposes, that they fearlessly preached Him to the world, even at the cost of their lives.

If the mystery of this feast were accomplished in our hearts, we should be sure to celebrate its outward ceremonies well. Were our souls watered with but one drop from the mighty river which flows from the throne of God and the Lamb, it would quench in us all thirst for anything in this world, and remove the aridity and hardness that make us so dry, tepid, and miserable. How grateful should we feel to our Savior for having redeemed us and blotted out our sins and given us perfect joy instead of sorrow! Suffering, exile, the absence from those we love, the want of things we now think necessary, or other trials would no longer afflict us. So powerful is the fire of the Holy Spirit that it mounts upward, and gives us a love and trust in God that no water of sorrow or affliction can extinguish; it remains ever alight; it fills and inflames our hearts, burning away all evil, so that not even death can conquer him whose evil passions it has destroyed.

This is the beloved Guest, who cured the wound that our Lord's departure made in the hearts of those who loved Him, and filled the place He had left empty. If the Paraclete could console them for the absence of Jesus, how much more can He comfort us in any grief caused by the loss of creatures! He is the Parent who cares so tenderly for the orphaned that He clothes them with power from on high and, sheltering them beneath His mantle, teaches them that there is One in Heaven whom they may dare, without presumption, to call their Father. He raises the fallen, enlightens our darkness, warms what is frozen, brings back the erring, refreshes the weary, and each day gives souls new strength to fly upward, even to the mount of God.

Surely such a wonderful gift should fill us with zeal and make us give all our hearts' affections to purchase this precious pearl, which is our true treasure, and which alone can make us happy. All around we hear the tidings of His coming to men and of His longing to dwell in their hearts. Let us not allow Him to pass by, but constrain Him to visit and comfort us that we may serve Him the better. He will need little entreaty; ask Him in our Lord's name, for the Father sends Him through Jesus Christ, His Son. It is our Savior who obtained for us poor mortal creatures, frail, impure, and subject to many evils though we be, the gift of the Holy Spirit, who is higher above us than the firmament is from the earth. Our vileness could never have attracted Him. Our Redeemer, the Only-Begotten of His Father in Heaven, abased Himself to become man on earth and, taking our weakness on Himself, suffered, toiled and gave His life, so that the Paraclete, the Creator of all things, might deign to come to us, poor vessels of clay.

Let us, then, thank our Savior, and rejoice in the fruit of His labors. Since, through His merits, the Holy Spirit wills to dwell within us, let us not be so ungrateful as to lose both of these favors, nor so foolish as to reject the Holy Spirit, who deigns to become our Father and our Guide. We should go forth with love, to meet Him who comes with love; we should feel an ardent longing to receive Him, for where He is much longed for, He gladly stays. Let us cry, with Isaiah: "My soul hath desired Thee in the night; yea, and with my spirit within me in the morning early I will watch to Thee."[118] That soul "desires" the Holy Spirit by night, which in the time of sorrow puts no confidence in itself, but sighs to Him, as the Comforter of the afflicted and the Solace of all in pain: it "watches for Him in the morning early," when its first care is to provide a dwelling for this divine Guest and to study how best to obtain this grace. If the Holy Spirit is thus eagerly desired and invoked, He will come, like our Lord, who was the Desired of all nations, and will assuredly enter our hearts, for He loves those who long to possess Him.

[118] Isa. 26:9.

Let us invite the Paraclete, then, by heart and voice, to dwell within us, and let us be sure we have some feast to offer Him when He comes. To please Him, we must destroy our fleshly passions, for He detests them; we must mortify our own judgment, so that we can be taught by Him, for two people cannot govern a house well unless the wiser take control. We must also renounce our own will, which is the chief enemy of the Holy Spirit, who teaches us to say "Not my will, but Thine be done."[119] Let us, too, cleanse our consciences by confession and penance from the slightest defilement, for this Heavenly Guest is a lover of purity, and there must be nothing to offend Him in the place where He lodges: we must keep peace both with ourselves and with others, for even quarrelsome people hide their dissensions before a guest whom they wish to honor.

When this mighty King deigns to make our hearts His palace, we should close them to all else and, being recollected in His presence, not let our minds leave Him to wander elsewhere. We should worship Him with the deepest reverence, assuring Him that nothing shall ever make us desert Him or be allowed to come between us. Then we shall enjoy Him as we ought, for He can give us a happiness of which nothing can deprive us. Then our sorrows shall be turned into joy, and we shall drink of the river of the delights of God until it inebriates us.

It will be a great consolation to me to know that you are in the hands of Him who will preserve, and teach, and save you eternally, and I beg of Him to take you under His protection.

---

[119] Luke 22:42.

25

To a Lady

———

On Pentecost and Corpus Christi—
the Link Between the Holy Spirit and the Eucharist

Dear Madam,

It would interest me to know what is passing in your soul during this week, which is consecrated to the Holy Spirit. He gives light to the understanding, love to the will, and even strength to the body, which gift is symbolized by the parable of the three loaves the man offered his friend, on returning hungry and weary from his journey. The Holy Spirit takes away the hunger our heart feels when wandering among creatures and fills it with the bread of fullness and satisfaction.

Woe to us if we feel not the nothingness of all that is visible and turn not to God, if only because we are wearied at discovering the defects and nothingness of all in which we hoped to find our rest. When, O God, will our souls be chaste and loyal to Christ our Spouse; when will our love, untainted by affection for any creature, be wholly given to Him? When shall we learn that He alone is the Master of our souls, that He created us for Himself, and that He alone can satisfy us? Can we not remember that we have often experienced how ill the world treats those who trust it, and that our souls have never known rest nor peace except, when, realizing their miseries and poverty, they have taken refuge in God and been received in His embrace? A short space of this joy is worth more than a lifetime spent in the empty noise and vanities of this foolish world. There can be no better time than this to say to earthly things "I know you not," and to cleanse and empty our souls, so as to provide a dwelling-place for the God who created us from nothingness.

The Paraclete who will visit us is so holy that He would not come even to the disciples until our Lord's Body was taken from their sight, to show how utterly empty must be the temple in which He dwells. I am glad that, having prepared your heart by His grace, you have received Him into it, both to His joy and your own. Rejoice with the Holy Spirit, for He is joy itself; remember how St. Paul tells us not to grieve "the Holy Spirit of God, whereby you are sealed unto the day of redemption,"[120] that is, the Last Judgment. To be dull and sad, to serve Him slothfully and tepidly, and to perform actions displeasing to this most holy Guest, is "to grieve the Holy Spirit."

He is "flame" and wishes His servant to be ardent and to glow with fervor and to throw onto the fire kindled in his heart the fuel of good works and light it up with holy thoughts. This will prevent this heavenly flame from dying out. Our spiritual vitality depends on its burning: if we keep it alive, it will maintain our life in God, although we are only returning to Him what He has first given us.

This week will have been a real feast to you, as you have kept not only its outward observances, with those who care for nothing but its ritual and festivities, but in your heart also, as God commands, who wishes us "to adore Him in spirit."[121]

Let us now consider how you are to prepare for the feast of Corpus Christi, which is so near at hand. It would indeed be a

[120] Eph. 4:30.
[121] John 4:23.

disgrace for the Christian soul not to long and hunger after this holy Bread. Christ was waited for even by the three kings in their far-off country and desired by the prophets and patriarchs long before the Incarnation. What greater joy than to see our Lord, whom heaven and earth cannot contain, veiled beneath the accidents of bread: sometimes borne by our hands, passing among us through our streets, and making Himself our companion, and again, sometimes deigning to enter into our poor sinful breasts.

Do not let my words pass from your mind, but rouse yourself to consider this great favor and work of God. Empty your heart of all else, that it may hunger keenly for this celestial Bread on which the angels feed. Be watchful during these days lest your attention wander. This is the week consecrated to the Holy Spirit; therefore, beg Him for grace to observe devoutly the feast of the Body of Christ. That Body was conceived by Him, and when we receive Holy Communion on that day, the Paraclete will come to us also, because it was through our Lord's merits that He was sent to us. Christ's merits are imparted to us in the Holy Eucharist in proportion to the worthiness of our dispositions.

Thus, one festival prepares us for the next and should make us long for it. Unlike the banquets of the world, where those who have feasted at noon are not hungry at night, each festival of the Church increases our appetite for the next, fulfilling God's promise in Leviticus: "The threshing of your harvest shall reach unto the vintage, and the vintage shall reach unto the sowing time; and you shall eat your bread to the full."[122]

Blessed be God, for so bountifully providing for us that He even bestows on us His very Self. The Son is given to us, and through Him the Holy Spirit, and with Them comes the Father. Thus, the Father, the Son, and the Holy Spirit reside within us, and we already have a beginning here of that communion with

[122] Lev. 26:5.

God which will be perfect in the next life. Let us thank Him for all His mercies and prepare ourselves to receive the favors that still remain to be bestowed on us. With hearts raised on high, let us celebrate the feasts of Heaven, so that from temporal joys we may pass to those which are eternal, in which I pray that you, Madam, may have your share. Amen.

An Invitation

Reader, the book that you hold in your hands was published by Sophia Institute Press.

Sophia Institute seeks to restore man's knowledge of eternal truth, including man's knowledge of his own nature, his relation to other persons, and his relation to God.

Our press fulfills this mission by offering translations, reprints, and new publications. We offer scholarly as well as popular publications; there are works of fiction along with books that draw from all the arts and sciences of our civilization. These books afford readers a rich source of the enduring wisdom of mankind.

Sophia Institute Press is the publishing arm of the Thomas More College of Liberal Arts and Holy Spirit College. Both colleges are dedicated to providing university-level education in the Western tradition under the guiding light of Catholic teaching.

If you know a young person who might be interested in the ideas found in this book, share it. If you know a young person seeking a college that takes seriously the adventure of learning and the quest for truth, bring our institutions to his attention.

www.SophiaInstitute.com
www.ThomasMoreCollege.edu
www.HolySpiritCollege.org

SOPHIA INSTITUTE PRESS

THE PUBLISHING DIVISION OF

Sophia Institute Press® is a registered trademark of Sophia Institute. Sophia Institute is a tax-exempt institution as defined by the Internal Revenue Code, Section 501(c)(3). Tax I.D. 22-2548708.